Beyond the Gantt Chart: The Human Element of Project Management Success Through Emotional Intelligence

Dr. Stefan Oborski (PMP)

Table of Contents

Introduction

Welcome, and thank you for purchasing **"Beyond the Gantt Chart: The Human Element of Project Management Success through Emotional Intelligence."** In this book, I aim to highlight the often overlooked yet immensely powerful superpower within every project manager and Project Management Office (PMO) leader— emotional intelligence. Drawing from my extensive experience in project management and leadership within project management offices, I have witnessed firsthand the remarkable impact that high and low emotional intelligence can have on project teams, clients, stakeholders, and the overall success of projects, project teams, and project managers' careers.

At the project level, emotional intelligence can truly make or break the dynamics within a team. When project managers possess a high level of emotional intelligence, they foster an environment of trust, empathy, and collaboration. Team members feel a sense of value, understanding, and motivation to give their best. On the other hand, a lack of emotional intelligence can lead to misunderstandings, conflicts, lack of trust, and reduced productivity, hindering project progress and ultimately costing the company time and money.

Imagine a project team facing a critical setback threatening their progress. A project manager with high emotional intelligence would understand the emotions and concerns of team members, offering support, reassurance, and guidance. By demonstrating empathy and clear communication, they help the team navigate the challenges, maintain morale, and ultimately achieve success. Conversely, a project manager lacking emotional intelligence might dismiss or ignore the team's emotional needs, amplifying stress and creating a toxic working environment.

Moving beyond the project level, emotional intelligence is equally vital for PMO leaders. A project management office is the driving force behind successful project execution throughout an organization.

Leaders with high emotional intelligence can effectively inspire, motivate, and align the project management team. They understand individuals' unique strengths and weaknesses, fostering a culture of growth and development. This, in turn, enhances the performance of the PMO, improves its perception within the organization, and amplifies customer satisfaction and profitability.

For project managers and PMO leaders, emotional intelligence is also necessary to navigate through their organizations successfully. Both project managers and PMO leaders must interact with finance for funding, HR for new hires, and throughout the organization to get people assigned to matrixed teams. Having high emotional intelligence can make this a much more efficient process by showing empathy and being able to negotiate outcomes that benefit all parties successfully.

I firmly believe that emotional intelligence is the secret ingredient that can elevate project management and PMO leadership to new heights. By putting emotional intelligence at the forefront, project managers and PMO leaders can cultivate high-performing teams, build stronger relationships with clients and stakeholders, and drive exceptional project outcomes. Emotional intelligence is not just a soft skill but a vital competency for project managers and PMO leaders to thrive, lead their teams effectively within organizations, and have successful careers. Here is the thing, emotional intelligence can be learned! In the following chapters, we will better understand emotional intelligence with actionable insights that will equip you with the tools to develop and enhance your emotional intelligence as a project manager or PMO leader. Let's bring emotional intelligence out of the shadows and empower ourselves to create impactful and successful projects.

Let the journey begin!

Self Assessment

Do you wonder where you may be as far as emotional intelligence? I have created this free, short project manager's emotional intelligence assessment. This self-assessment is specifically tailored for project managers and can be the starting point for your emotional intelligence journey. It will show you some areas where you excel or may need to put some attention on.. Regardless, it will get you thinking about how emotional intelligence impacts project management.

You can download this free assessment HERE.

Link for print book:

https://theemotionallyintelligentpm.lpages.co/the-pm-30-question-eq-assessment

What is Emotional Intelligence?

Emotional intelligence, often abbreviated as EQ or EI, is a concept that has gained significant recognition in various fields, including psychology, leadership, education, and even business. Now it is time to get emotional intelligence the respect it deserves in project management! Emotional intelligence is the ability to recognize, handle, and apply emotions effectively, both in oneself and with other people.

The Five Pillars of Emotional Intelligence:

To fully comprehend emotional intelligence, it is essential to explore its five pillars introduced by Peter Salovey and John D. Mayer in the early 1990s. Each pillar represents a crucial aspect of emotional intelligence development. These pillars are:

1. Self-awareness:

At the foundation of emotional intelligence lies self-awareness, which involves recognizing and being aware of one's emotions, thoughts, and behaviors. Individuals with a high level of self-awareness possess a deep understanding of their strengths and weaknesses, as well as their emotional triggers and reactions. They are attuned to how their feelings influence their decisions and actions, which enables them to make better choices and navigate life's challenges more effectively.

Cultivating self-awareness involves self-reflection, mindfulness, and being open to feedback from others. Engaging in practices like meditation or journaling can facilitate the development of self-awareness by encouraging individuals to explore their inner thoughts and emotions in a non-judgmental manner. By acknowledging and accepting their emotions, people can harness the power of self-awareness to initiate personal growth and enhance their overall well-being.

2. Self-control (Emotional Regulation):

Once individuals become aware of their emotions, the next step in emotional intelligence is learning to control them appropriately. Self-control, also known as emotional regulation, refers to managing and channeling your emotions constructively, even in challenging situations. People with high emotional intelligence can prevent impulsive reactions to negative emotions and avoid being overwhelmed by intense feelings like anger, anxiety, or sadness.

Developing self-control involves recognizing emotional triggers and finding healthy ways to deal with them. Techniques like taking deep breaths, pausing and counting to ten, or taking a brief break in a stressful situation can assist you to regain composure. Furthermore, practicing empathy towards oneself and understanding that it's acceptable to have a wide range of emotions can aid in maintaining emotional well-being. By honing their self-control, individuals can foster better decision-making, build resilience, and maintain harmonious relationships.

3. Social Awareness (Empathy):

Social awareness, often referred to as empathy, centers around the capacity to understand and empathize with the emotions from other people's points of view. Empathetic individuals are attuned to the feelings of those around them, which enables them to respond compassionately and navigate social interactions with sensitivity. Empathy is a powerful tool for fostering connection and building trust in any relationship.

Cultivating empathy involves active listening and understanding others' feelings without judgment. Understanding from another person's view allows individuals to develop a deeper appreciation for diverse perspectives, fostering a sense of connection and mutual understanding. Empathy also involves respecting the emotions of others, even if they differ from one's own. Individuals can create a more inclusive and supportive social environment by embracing social awareness.

4. Relationship Management:

The fourth pillar of emotional intelligence is relationship management, which encompasses building and maintaining healthy, fulfilling relationships with others. This skill involves effective communication, conflict resolution, and collaboration, which are essential for thriving in both personal and professional settings.

Effective relationship management involves open and honest communication, active listening, and the ability to express oneself while taking into consideration the feelings of others. Conflict resolution skills are crucial in managing disagreements constructively, fostering compromise, and finding solutions that benefit all parties involved. Moreover, individuals with strong relationship management skills can adapt their communication styles to different contexts and personalities, leading to smoother interactions and strengthened connections.

5. Motivation:

The final pillar of emotional intelligence is motivation, which refers to harnessing and maintaining the drive to bring about personal and professional goals. Motivated individuals are self-starters who challenge and set-back head-on. A sense of purpose drives them and continuously seek self-improvement and growth.

Intrinsic motivation, the motivation that arises from within oneself, is particularly valuable for fostering emotional intelligence. By identifying personal values and aligning goals with these values, individuals can tap into a wellspring of inner motivation. Setting realistic and achievable goals, celebrating progress, and viewing setbacks as opportunities for learning are strategies that can bolster motivation and sustain progress over time.

The Impact of Emotional Intelligence:

Emotional intelligence plays a crucial role in various aspects of life, influencing personal well-being, professional success, and the quality of relationships. Individuals with high emotional intelligence are better equipped to manage stress, adapt to change, and handle conflicts effectively. Moreover, emotional intelligence is an essential aspect of effective leadership, as it enables leaders to understand and motivate their teams, foster a positive work environment, and inspire collaboration and innovation.

Furthermore, emotional intelligence is closely linked to mental health and overall satisfaction with life. People with higher levels of emotional intelligence tend to experience lower levels of anxiety and depression and have a more positive outlook on life. Additionally, emotional intelligence is associated with greater social support and a higher sense of belonging, which contributes to a more fulfilling and enriching social life.

Emotional intelligence is a multifaceted concept that encompasses self-awareness, self-control, social awareness, relationship management, and motivation. It equips individuals to understand and handle their emotions effectively, fostering personal growth and improved well-being. Moreover, emotional intelligence plays a pivotal role in social interactions, enabling individuals to empathize with others, build meaningful relationships, and thrive in various social settings.

Developing emotional intelligence is a never-ending journey that involves self-reflection, self-compassion, and a commitment to growth. By cultivating these five pillars, individuals can enhance their emotional intelligence and harness its power to navigate life's challenges, foster healthy relationships, and positively impact the world around them. Embracing emotional intelligence not only benefits individuals personally but also contributes to a more empathetic, understanding, and harmonious society as a whole.

The Importance of Emotional Intelligence in Project Management

Effective project management is not solely about technical expertise and cost, schedule, and performance adherence. It is also about understanding, motivating, and collaborating with individuals within the project team and stakeholders. Emotional intelligence plays a pivotal role in successful project management, as it empowers project managers and PMO leaders to navigate through the complexities of human interactions, harness team dynamics, and cultivate a conducive work environment. Let's explore a bit deeper why emotional intelligence is such a crucial skill for project managers and PMO leaders

1. Emotionally Intelligent Communication

One of the fundamental aspects of project management is effective communication. Project managers communicate at team meetings, stakeholder updates, project status updates, and constant emails and phone calls. In fact, some studies have suggested that project managers spend up to 75-90% of their time communicating. Emotional intelligence enables project managers to communicate with empathy, active listening, and sensitivity to the emotional state of team members. By acknowledging and understanding emotions, project managers can tailor their communication styles to motivate, inspire, and resolve conflicts within the team.

Example: During a high-pressure project, a team member struggles to meet a deadline due to personal issues. An emotionally intelligent project manager engages in a private conversation with the team member, demonstrating empathy and offering support and flexibility to help them overcome the challenge.

2. Conflict Resolution and Collaboration

In any project, conflicts are inevitable. Emotional intelligence empowers project managers to manage conflicts constructively rather than not addressing them or escalating them. By recognizing and addressing emotions involved in the conflict, the project manager can promote a collaborative environment, foster open discussions, and facilitate the resolution process.

Example: Two team members have a disagreement regarding the project's way forward. An emotionally intelligent project manager holds a facilitated discussion, allowing each member to express their viewpoints and emotions. Through active listening and empathetic understanding, the manager guides the team to find a mutually beneficial solution.

3. Leadership and Motivation

Project managers with high emotional intelligence are better equipped to lead and motivate their teams. They can identify the unique strengths and weaknesses of team members and utilize this knowledge to delegate tasks effectively. By recognizing and praising achievements, emotionally intelligent leaders boost team morale, leading to increased commitment and productivity.

Example: A project manager equipped with emotional intelligence notices that one team member is passionate about data analysis. The manager assigns them a crucial data-driven task, acknowledging their expertise, which enhances the team member's motivation and commitment to the project.

4. Adaptability and Resilience

Projects are subject to unexpected changes and challenges. Emotionally intelligent project managers can adapt to shifting circumstances, maintaining composure in stressful situations. They are more resilient in the face of obstacles, helping them bounce back and keep the project on track.

Example: A project manager faces significant delays due to external factors beyond their control. Demonstrating emotional intelligence, the manager communicates the situation transparently to the stakeholders, reassures the team, and works collaboratively to devise a revised plan that accounts for the challenges.

5. Stakeholder Management

A successful project hinges on effective stakeholder management. Emotionally intelligent project managers can anticipate the needs and concerns of stakeholders, build stronger relationships, and manage expectations proactively.

Example: An emotionally intelligent PMO leader, while presenting the project progress to stakeholders, not only focuses on data and metrics but also acknowledges the stakeholders' emotional investment in the project. They address potential concerns and demonstrate empathy, ensuring a positive and trusting relationship with the stakeholders.

6. Emotional Resonance and Team Cohesion

Emotionally intelligent project managers foster a sense of emotional resonance within the team, creating a cohesive and supportive work environment. When team members feel valued and understood, they are more likely to collaborate, share knowledge, and support each other's growth.

Example: During a challenging phase of the project, an emotionally intelligent project manager organizes team-building activities, encouraging team members to share personal stories and experiences. This emotional connection enhances team cohesion and boosts morale.

7. Self-Management and Personal Growth

Emotional intelligence also involves understanding one's emotions and managing them effectively. Project managers with high emotional intelligence can control their stress, maintain focus, and make rational decisions even in high-pressure situations. Additionally, they actively seek feedback and reflect on their performance to continuously improve.

Example: After facing criticism from stakeholders about project delays, an emotionally intelligent project manager refrains from reacting impulsively. Instead, they take a step back, analyze the situation, seek feedback from the team, and implement changes to prevent similar issues in the future.

As you can see, emotional intelligence is an indispensable skill for project managers and PMO leaders. It empowers them to communicate effectively, resolve conflicts, motivate teams, adapt to challenges, manage stakeholders, promote team cohesion, and grow both personally and professionally. <u>Project management is more than just task coordination. It involves skillfully managing people, emotions, and relationships.</u> By nurturing emotional intelligence, project managers can foster a positive and productive work environment, leading to successful project delivery and long-term organizational success. As the business landscape evolves, emotional intelligence will remain a key differentiator for exceptional project management and leadership.

Misconceptions About Emotional Intelligence

A misconception is a false or inaccurate belief held by individuals or a group of people about a particular subject, concept, or phenomenon. These beliefs are often based on incomplete information, misinterpretation of facts, cultural biases, or preconceived notions. Misconceptions can be widespread and deeply ingrained in society, leading many to accept them as truth without questioning their validity.

One of the significant characteristics of misconceptions is that they stand in contrast to well-established evidence or widely accepted knowledge. As a result, they can hinder people from understanding the truth or adopting more accurate beliefs. Misconceptions may arise in various fields, including science, history, culture, and personal opinions.

When individuals hold onto misconceptions, it can harm their lives and influence their decision-making processes. For example, a false belief about their abilities, skills, or worth can lead to limiting beliefs. These limiting beliefs can prevent them from realizing their full potential, taking on new challenges, or pursuing their goals.

Self-doubt is another common consequence of misconceptions. If someone internalizes false beliefs about themselves or their abilities, they may constantly doubt their ability to succeed or overcome obstacles. This self-doubt can create a negative feedback loop, where individuals avoid taking risks or challenging themselves, thus reinforcing the limitations imposed by the misconceptions.

Misconceptions can also result in stagnation, both on a personal level and in society. Progress and growth become complicated when people resist accepting new information or ideas because they cling to false beliefs. In scientific fields, for instance, the persistence of misconceptions can hinder knowledge development and impede advancements.

Addressing misconceptions is crucial for personal growth. Encouraging critical thinking, open-mindedness, and a willingness to question one's beliefs can help individuals overcome misconceptions. In educational settings, teachers and educators play a vital role in dispelling misconceptions and fostering a deeper understanding of various subjects.

To combat misconceptions effectively, promoting a culture of curiosity, evidence-based thinking, and a willingness to update beliefs in the face of new information is essential. By doing so, individuals can liberate themselves from limiting beliefs, self-doubt, and stagnation, enabling personal and collective growth and progress.

Here are some common misconceptions about emotional intelligence.

1. Emotional intelligence is a fixed trait and cannot be developed or improved.

-This is FALSE and perhaps the biggest misconception about emotional intelligence. Emotional Intelligence is a learnable trait, and this course is just a start to gaining more knowledge and improving your emotional intelligence prowess.

2. Emotional intelligence only applies to specific individuals or personality types.

-This is FALSE and goes with the first misconception. Emotional Intelligence is for everyone, and anyone can learn these valuable skills

3. Emotional intelligence is solely about being able to understand and manage your own emotions.

-This is FALSE; managing your emotions is vital to emotional intelligence. However, it is only part of it. As we will learn, understanding others' emotions is also essential to having high emotional intelligence skills.

4. Emotional intelligence is only vital in personal relationships and irrelevant to the workplace.

-This is FALES. Anywhere there are dealings with people and relationships, at work, at home, at the dry cleaners... emotional intelligence has a valuable place.

5. Emotional intelligence is optional for successful leadership or management.

-This is FALSE. The higher you get in leadership, the more people you deal with and the more influence you need. Emotional intelligence is vital to that effort.

6. Emotional intelligence is a soft skill and does not contribute to professional success.

-Yes, emotional Intelligence is not only a soft skill but the foundation of all the other soft skills. Given that, it is a significant factor in professional success. As an aspiring professional and project manager, you have to be able to communicate with your boss and peers and build trust. You need to have those skills to be held back. If you have these skills, you will rise above the rest and climb the promotional ladder.

7. Emotional intelligence can be developed overnight or with a quick fix.

-This is FALSE. Emotional intelligence takes work and practice. This book is an excellent step toward emotional intelligence improvement, but it is just the beginning.

8. Emotional intelligence is only relevant in face-to-face interactions, not digital communication.

-This is FALSE. In today's remote world, emotional intelligence is even more critical. You cannot just go down to the water cooler and build relationships. On a Zoom call, it is harder to read body language.

However, emotional intelligence skills can be displayed in today's remote environment

9. Emotional intelligence is a buzzword or fad with no scientific basis.

-This is FALES. There have been many studies done supporting the validity of emotional intelligence. For example, A study published in the Journal of Organizational Behavior discovered that teams with high emotional intelligence outperformed those with low emotional intelligence.

10. Emotional intelligence is less important than intellectual intelligence for overall success.

-This is FALSE. Smarts will only get you so far. You have to be able to communicate with people effectively, get your message across and influence them on your idea or action.

By acknowledging and discarding these misconceptions, we are on the way to our own personal and intellectual growth. Embracing a mindset of continuous learning and open-mindedness allows us to move forward with a clearer understanding of the world, unburdened by the limitations of false beliefs that others may have laid before us regarding emotional intelligence. Let us now embrace the pursuit of knowledge and strive for a more enlightened and empowered future in our project management mindset.

Emotions are complicated

Emotions are complicated because they arise from biological, psychological, and social factors. Several reasons contribute to the complexity of emotions:

❖ **1. Multifactorial Origin:** Emotions are not solely a result of one cause but a combination of various factors.

16

Biological factors, such as brain chemistry and hormonal changes, play a significant role. Still, external stimuli, past experiences, cultural influences, and individual personality traits also contribute to how emotions are experienced and expressed.

❖ **Subjectivity:** Emotions are subjective experiences that are unique to each individual. The same event or situation can evoke different emotional responses in other people due to their personal perspectives, beliefs, and past experiences.

❖ **Ambiguity:** Emotions can be ambiguous and difficult to pinpoint accurately. Sometimes, a person may experience mixed emotions simultaneously, making it challenging to identify and interpret each emotion separately.

❖ **Emotional Regulation:** People vary in their ability to regulate and manage emotions. Some individuals may be naturally more emotionally reactive, while others may have learned coping mechanisms to control their emotional responses.

❖ **Social and Cultural Context:** Social norms, cultural values, and group expectations influence how emotions are conveyed and understood. Different social groups may encourage or discourage specific emotional behavior, leading to varied emotional expressions across societies.

❖ **Cognitive Appraisal:** How people interpret and appraise situations can influence their emotional responses. Two individuals facing the same event may feel differently based on their interpretations of its significance and meaning.

❖ **Developmental Changes:** Emotions can evolve and change over time as individuals mature and gain new life experiences. What may have triggered intense emotions in the past may have a different impact later in life.

❖ **Defense Mechanisms:** Sometimes, individuals may unconsciously use defense mechanisms to protect themselves from a flood of incoming emotions. These mechanisms can alter how emotions are perceived or expressed.

To illustrate how each of us can feel emotions differently, consider a scenario where a group of people receives the news that their company is downsizing and some employees will lose their jobs:

Person A: May feel devastated and fearful about potential unemployment, experiencing anxiety and sadness.

Person B: Might feel angry and resentful, perceiving the layoff as an unfair decision by the management.

Person C: Could feel relieved and hopeful, viewing the layoff as an opportunity to pursue a career change they've been considering.

Person D: May initially feel shocked and become determined to work harder to prove their worth and avoid being laid off.

These varied emotional responses arise due to each individual's unique personality traits, coping mechanisms, past experiences with job security, perceptions of the company culture, and outlook on the future.

Understanding and respecting the complexity of emotions is crucial for building empathy and effective communication with others. It reminds us that each person's emotional experience is valid and influenced by a complex interplay of individual and situational factors.

In the context of project management, emotions can significantly impact a project manager's ability to lead effectively and manage various challenges. Here's how a project manager might react to specific scenarios:

1. Dealing with a Difficult Customer: When facing a demanding customer, a project manager may experience various emotions, such as frustration, anxiety, or anger. How they manage these emotions will influence their ability to find a resolution. Remaining calm and empathetic can help de-escalate the situation and foster a more constructive dialogue.

2. Handling an Unaccepted Deliverable: If stakeholders do not accept a project deliverable, the project manager might feel disappointment or even a sense of failure. They need to acknowledge these emotions while focusing on identifying the issues, understanding stakeholder expectations, and developing a plan to address the concerns effectively.

3. Dealing with a Difficult Team Member: Interactions with challenging team members can evoke irritation or helplessness. A project manager must address any issues promptly but also with emotional intelligence, striving to understand the underlying reasons for the team member's behavior and constructively finding ways to resolve conflicts.

4. Responding to Project Setbacks: Project managers may face setbacks, unexpected challenges, or failures, leading to emotions like stress, disappointment, or doubt. Project managers must cope with these emotions effectively, maintain resilience, and rally the team to find alternative solutions.

Emotions are powerful forces that influence human behavior and decision-making in virtually all aspects of life, including project management. Project managers must recognize, understand, and manage emotions to lead effectively, maintain team morale, and navigate challenges successfully. Emotional intelligence is crucial in helping project managers react constructively and build positive working relationships with stakeholders, team members, and clients.

Core Emotions

People experience various emotions, each with unique qualities and significance. While emotions can be complex and blend together, here are some of the core emotions that people commonly feel:

1. **Happiness/Joy:** A positive and uplifting emotion experienced when one feels content, elated, or satisfied. Accomplishments, pleasant experiences, or the presence of loved ones can trigger it.

2. **Sadness/Grief:** An emotion tied to loss, disappointment, or feeling downhearted. Sadness can arise from various situations, such as the death of a friend or family member, failure, or loneliness.

3. **Fear:** An innate emotion that alerts us to potential threats or dangers. Fear can be rational, like being scared of a dangerous animal, or irrational, like specific phobias.

4. **Anger/Rage:** A strong emotional response to perceived injustices, frustrations, or provocations. Anger can lead to intense reactions and, if not managed properly, can result in destructive behavior.

5. **Disgust:** A reaction to something unpleasant, offensive, or repulsive. It helps protect us from harmful substances or situations.

6. **Surprise:** The sudden and unexpected reaction to something out of the ordinary. Surprise can be positive or negative, and it often elicits immediate attention.

7. **Anticipation:** The feeling of excitement and expectation when looking forward to the future or an event.

8. **Trust:** An emotional state where one believes in the reliability, honesty, and goodwill of others.

9. **Doubt/Insecurity:** Feeling uncertain or lacking confidence in oneself or a situation.

10. **Love/Affection is** characterized by strong feelings for, watchfulness over, and affection towards someone or something.

11. **Regret:** Sorrow or remorse over past actions or missed opportunities.

12. **Jealousy:** A mix of fear, insecurity, and envy when one feels someone has something they do not.

13. **Pride:** A sense of satisfaction and self-worth from achievements, abilities, or associations.

14. **Shame/Embarrassment:** The emotion associated with feeling exposed or humiliated, often due to violating social norms or expectations.

15. **Hope:** The optimistic outlook for positive outcomes in the future, even during hard and difficult times.

These core emotions form the foundation of human experiences and play a crucial role in framing how we see things, our actions, and our interactions with others and the world around us. As social beings, our ability to recognize, understand, and manage these emotions influences our emotional intelligence and the quality of our relationships with others.

Emotions Are Contagious

Emotions are the center of being human and can significantly impact the success of a project. As a project manager, understanding the contagious nature of emotions and how they can affect the team is crucial for promoting a positive and productive work environment.

The Contagious Nature of Emotions

Emotions are contagious, meaning they can spread from one individual to another within a team or an organization. This phenomenon occurs through non-verbal cues, body language, facial expressions, and even tone of voice. As a project manager, your emotional state can influence the overall mood and dynamics of the team, leading to either positive or negative outcomes.

Positive Emotions

A. Enthusiasm: When a project manager exhibits enthusiasm and excitement about the project's goals and milestones, team members are more likely to feel motivated and energized. This positive emotion can lead to increased interactions and a higher level of commitment to achieving project success.

Example: James, a project manager, is passionate about the project he is leading. During team meetings, he shares his enthusiasm for the project's impact on customers and the company. As a result, the team feels inspired and becomes more willing to go the extra mile to deliver outstanding results.

B. Confidence: Project managers who display confidence in their team's abilities and express belief in their capacity to overcome challenges can boost team members' self-assurance. This positive emotional state encourages individuals to take risks and embrace innovative solutions.

Example: Sarah, a project manager, faces a critical issue during a project. Instead of panicking, she remains calm and trusts the team's problem-solving skills. Her confidence influences the team, and together they collaboratively find a creative solution to the problem.

C. Gratitude: Showing appreciation for the team's hard work and dedication fosters a positive emotional climate. Gratitude can strengthen the bond between team members and the project manager, increasing job satisfaction and loyalty.

Example: As the project reaches its final stages, Emily, the project manager, gathers the team to express her sincere gratitude for their efforts. She acknowledges each team member's efforts and praises their achievements, instilling a sense of pride and accomplishment in the team.

Negative Emotions

A. Stress and Anxiety: Project managers who frequently display stress and anxiety can inadvertently transfer these emotions to the team. This negative emotional state can decrease productivity, lower team morale, and potential burnout.

Example: Michael, a project manager, is constantly under pressure due to tight project deadlines. His stress levels affect the team, increasing tension and reducing collaboration among members.

B. Frustration: A project manager's frustration and irritation can create a toxic work environment. Team members may become unmotivated and not have confidence in their abilities.

Example: Jessica, a project manager, is frustrated with the project's slow progress. Her impatience is evident during team meetings, which causes team members to feel disheartened and fearful of sharing any setbacks.

C. Indifference: A project manager who appears disinterested or indifferent can negatively impact team motivation and engagement. Team members may question the significance of their work and lose their interest in the project.

Example: David, a project manager, rarely acknowledges the team's efforts and, even more, rarely provides feedback. This lack of interest leads to a decline in team morale and a decrease in the quality of work the team produces.

Managing Contagious Emotions

Recognizing the contagious nature of emotions is essential for project managers. To foster a positive emotional culture within the team, project managers can employ various strategies:

1. Self-awareness: Project managers must be aware of their emotional states and how they might influence the team. Self-reflection and emotional intelligence can help project managers manage their emotions effectively.

2. Communication: Open and honest communication with the team can help project managers proactively address any emotional challenges or concerns. Encouraging team members to convey their emotions and concerns can prevent negative emotions from festering.

3. Positive reinforcement: Celebrating successes, offering praise, and showing appreciation for the team's efforts can nurture positive emotions and boost team morale.

4. Problem-solving orientation: Encouraging a problem-solving mindset helps the team focus on finding solutions rather than dwelling on negative emotions caused by setbacks.

5.   Emotional support: Project managers can provide emotional support to team members during challenging times, fostering a sense of camaraderie and trust.

As a project manager, your emotional state can significantly impact the team's performance and well-being. Project managers can create a thriving and productive work environment by fostering positive emotions such as enthusiasm, confidence, and gratitude. Likewise, being mindful of negative emotions such as stress, frustration, and indifference can help project managers address issues before they become detrimental to the project's success. Managing contagious emotions is essential for project managers seeking to lead high-performing and motivated teams.

The Mind-Body Connection

The connection between the mind and body is a fundamental aspect of human existence, deeply rooted in our evolutionary history. It is a dynamic relationship where emotions, thoughts, and physical sensations intricately interplay, shaping our experiences and overall well-being. This mind-body connection has been a crucial survival mechanism for humans throughout history and continues to play a significant role in how we navigate the world today.

Emotions are an essential part of being human. They encompass many experiences, from joy and love to fear and anger. These emotions are not merely abstract concepts confined to consciousness; tangible physical reactions within our bodies accompany them. Understanding the emotional mind-body connection is essential in comprehending how humans have thrived and survived since the earliest days of our existence.

One of the most primal emotions that shows the mind-body connection is fear. Like other emotions, fear is not just a feeling that occurs in isolation but rather a mind/body experience involving various physiological and psychological responses. When we

25

encounter what we perceive as a threatening situation, the fear response triggers a cascade of reactions throughout our system, preparing us for the "fight or flight" response.

The fight or flight response is a survival mechanism deeply ingrained in our existence. It dates back to the early days of humankind when our ancestors faced numerous threats in the wild, from predatory animals to natural disasters. In such life-threatening situations, the fear emotion would surge, alerting the body to react instantaneously for self-preservation.

When fear arises, the brain's amygdala, a key player in processing emotions, perceives the threat and activates the sympathetic nervous system. This, in turn, leads to the body's release of stress hormones like adrenaline and cortisol into the bloodstream, getting the body into action. The heart rate increases, blood pressure rises, and blood flow is redirected from less vital functions to the muscles, allowing the body to be primed for either fight or flight.

As humans advanced, this fight-or-flight response proved invaluable in overcoming challenges and ensuring survival. In times of imminent danger, individuals had to rely on quick and instinctual decisions to navigate threatening situations effectively. Whether facing a predator or defending against rival tribes, our ancestors' ability to harness this emotional mind-body connection was instrumental in their ability to adapt and thrive in harsh environments.

Over time, the human brain and body became intricately attuned to emotional responses, refining this survival mechanism. While the threats modern humans face have significantly changed from those of our ancestors, the emotional mind-body connection remains vital to human functioning. Nowadays, the "threats" are often more abstract and psychological, such as stress at work, financial worries, or social anxieties. In project management, the same response could come from a bad customer review, a hostile worker, or a lack of funding. Has the fight-or-flight response happened to you during a project?

Beyond the fight or flight response, the mind-body connection extends to other emotional experiences. For instance, happiness and joy are accompanied by the release of neurotransmitters like dopamine and endorphins, which help create these feelings. Similarly, feelings of love and connection are associated with releasing oxytocin, often called the "love hormone," which fosters social bonding and affection.

Moreover, the mind-body connection is vital in managing chronic illnesses and overall health. The field of psychoneuroimmunology explores how psychological factors, such as stress and emotions, can influence the immune system's functioning. Research in this field has shown that constant stress and negative emotions can seriously impact the immune system, making individuals more susceptible to various illnesses.

Conversely, positive emotions and a healthy mental state can have a protective effect on physical health. Studies have found that individuals who experience positive emotions more frequently tend to have better cardiovascular health, lower inflammation levels, and improved overall well-being. This highlights how the emotional mind-body connection can significantly impact our physical health and resilience.

In addition to physiological responses, emotions influence our behaviors and decision-making processes. Our emotional state can affect our cognitive abilities, memory, and attention, shaping how we interpret and respond to the situations around us. For example, a person in a state of fear may become hyper-vigilant and more attentive to potential threats, while someone experiencing joy may be more open to social interactions and bonding.

The emotional mind-body connection is a deeply ingrained aspect of human existence, dating back to our earliest ancestors. Emotions are not abstract concepts but dynamic experiences involving the intricate interplay between our minds and bodies. The fight or flight response, triggered by the emotion of fear, is a vivid example of how this connection has been crucial for human survival throughout history.

As our understanding of the mind-body connection continues to evolve, we gain deeper insights into how our emotional experiences shape our physical sensations, behaviors, and overall well-being. This knowledge has significant implications for mental health, physical health, and our ability to navigate the challenges and joys of life in the modern world. By recognizing and harnessing the power of the mind/body connection, we can strive to achieve greater harmony between our emotional and physical selves, leading to a more fulfilling and balanced existence.

Emotional Intelligence and Personality Assessments

Emotion and personality are closely intertwined. While distinct, they interact and influence each other in various ways.

1.   Relationship between Emotion and Personality:

Emotion refers to the complex psychological and physiological reactions that respond to external or internal stimuli. It involves feelings such as joy, fear, anger, sadness, and many others. Emotions are often brief and intense experiences that can change rapidly based on different situations and triggers.

On the flip side, personality refers to the heart-felt patterns of thoughts, emotions, and behaviors that distinguish an individual over time. It is the relatively stable and consistent aspect of a person's psychological nature. Personality traits describe how a person behaves and perceives the world.

The relationship between emotion and personality can be seen in several ways:

a. Emotional expression: Personality traits can influence how individuals express and experience emotions. For example, extroverted people might be more expressive and outgoing in showing their emotions, while introverted people might be more reserved.

b. Emotional regulation: Personality traits can impact an individual's ability to control emotions effectively. Some personalities might have a natural inclination towards emotional stability, while others might be more prone to experiencing intense emotional fluctuations.

c. Emotional tendencies: Certain personality traits are associated with specific emotional tendencies. For instance, a person with a neurotic personality might be more susceptible to anxiety and worry, while someone with high agreeableness might be more empathetic and compassionate.

d. Emotional development: Emotions can shape and influence an individual's personality over time. Repeated emotional experiences can contribute to forming certain personality traits and behaviors.

2.   Personality Assessment and Emotional Intelligence:

Personality assessments, such as the Color Code, can provide valuable insights into an individual's character, tendencies, and behavioral patterns. These assessments can also indirectly help increase emotional intelligence, which is the ability to recognize, understand, and manage one's own emotions and the emotions of others.

Here's how a personality assessment can contribute to the development of emotional intelligence:

a. Self-awareness: Personality assessments can offer individuals a deeper understanding of their strengths, weaknesses, and behavioral tendencies. This self-awareness is fundamental to emotional intelligence as it allows individuals to recognize their emotional triggers and patterns.

b. Empathy: Understanding one's personality traits can make empathizing with others' perspectives and emotions easier. When you know yourself better, you can relate to others more effectively and provide emotional support when needed.

c. Emotional Regulation: Personality assessments might shed light on specific traits that influence emotional regulation. By identifying potential challenges in managing emotions, individuals can work on growing healthy coping strategies and emotional resilience.

d. Communication: A personality assessment can provide insights into communication styles, preferences, and potential conflict areas in interpersonal relationships. This knowledge can lead to more effective communication and better handling of emotional situations.

e. Relationship building: Emotional intelligence is essential for building and maintaining healthy relationships. Understanding one's personality traits can improve social interactions and more profound connections.

The color code personality assessment is a popular tool used to identify and categorize different personality types based on four primary colors: Red, Yellow, Blue, and White. Each color represents specific traits, behaviors, and motivations.

- Red: The Red personality type is characterized by dominance, assertiveness, and a strong desire for control and achievement. Reds are natural leaders who are results-oriented, practical, and decisive. They are often competitive, driven, and have a no-nonsense approach to problem-solving. Reds prefer to take charge and may be seen as assertive or demanding in their interactions.

- Yellow: The Yellow personality type is outgoing, sociable, and enthusiastic. Yellows are often the life of the party, enjoying social interactions and forming connections with others. They are creative, optimistic, and spontaneous, enthusiastically embracing new experiences. Yellows are typically persuasive and tend to inspire and motivate those around them.

- Blue: The Blue personality type is characterized by empathy, sensitivity, and a relationship focus. Blues are natural caregivers and are deeply concerned about the well-being of others. They are supportive, nurturing, and value harmonious interactions. Blues are often good listeners willing to provide emotional support to those in need.

   ▪   White: The White personality type is calm, analytical, and reserved. Whites seek peace, stability, and a sense of order. They are detail-oriented, cautious decision-makers who prefer to think things through before acting. Whites are often seen as objective and diplomatic, valuing fairness and impartiality.

It's essential to note that most individuals possess a combination of these traits, and no color represents a superior or inferior personality type. The color code assessment provides insight into one's predominant characteristics and communication styles to enhance self-awareness and improve interactions with others. Understanding these color-coded personalities can be valuable in various settings, including personal relationships, team dynamics, and leadership roles.

Get started on your free personality assessment here: http://www.colorcode.com/coupon/EPTEI

*It is fun, and this link comes with a $10 off coupon if you choose to get the entire assessment.

I would be interested to hear what you thought of the assessment. You can contact me at: stefan@theemotionallyintelligentPM.com. I am looking forward to hearing about your results!

Benefits of Emotional Intelligence

In the realm of project management, possessing high levels of emotional intelligence can be a game-changer, offering many advantages that extend beyond traditional project management skills. By honing the ability to recognize, understand, and manage emotions—both their own and those of team members—project managers with heightened emotional intelligence can create a dynamic and harmonious work environment, effectively navigate challenges, and foster enhanced team collaboration. The benefits of this invaluable trait can significantly impact project outcomes and contribute to long-term success. Let's discuss a few advantages that high levels of emotional intelligence can bring.

Relationship Management

Project management is more than just task coordination and resource allocation. At its core, it involves managing people and relationships effectively. Building strong connections with members of the project team, project stakeholders, and clients is essential for a project to be successful. Emotional intelligence plays a pivotal role in relationship management, enabling project managers to navigate challenges, communicate effectively, and inspire their teams. In this chapter, we will explore the importance of emotional intelligence in relationship management for project managers and how it enhances project outcomes.

The Significance of Relationship Management in Project Management

1. **Enhanced Team Cohesion:** Project managers must lead diverse teams with different skills and personalities. Building positive relationships fosters trust and cooperation among team members, promoting a harmonious work environment that improves team cohesion and performance.

2. **Stakeholder Satisfaction:** Projects involve many stakeholders. Each stakeholder also brings with them unique expectations, interests, and personalities. An emotionally intelligent project manager can engage stakeholders effectively, understand their needs, and manage their expectations, leading to increased stakeholder satisfaction.

3. **Conflict Resolution:** Conflicts are bound to occur in any project. Emotional intelligence equips project managers with the skills to handle conflicts with sensitivity and empathy, seeking resolutions that satisfy all parties involved.

4. **Effective Communication:** Clear and open communication is vital for successful project outcomes. Emotional intelligence helps project managers communicate effectively, ensuring that information is conveyed accurately and understood by all team members and stakeholders.

5. **Motivated and Engaged Teams:** Emotionally intelligent project managers can energize and motivate their teams, fostering a sense of purpose and devotion to the project's success.

Stress management

In the fast-paced and demanding world of project management, professionals often grapple with high stress and pressure. Managing complex tasks, tight deadlines, and diverse teams can be overwhelming, leading to burnout, reduced productivity, and even sometimes health issues. However, amidst the chaos, one crucial skill can significantly alleviate stress and enhance overall performance: emotional intelligence. This chapter explores how emotional intelligence empowers project managers to navigate stress and foster a healthy work environment that promotes productivity, collaboration, and project success.

Stress is a natural response to challenging situations, but emotional intelligence enables project managers to recognize stress early on and respond effectively, preventing it from escalating.

The connection between emotional intelligence and stress management

Identifying Stress Triggers

High emotional intelligence enables project managers to identify their stress triggers more accurately. By being self-aware, they can recognize specific situations, tasks, or interactions that lead to increased stress levels. With this knowledge, project managers can proactively plan and implement strategies to effectively minimize or cope with these triggers.

Emotion Regulation

Project managers with strong emotional intelligence possess better emotion regulation skills. They can maintain their composure during crises, make intelligent decisions, and avoid spur-of-the-moment reactions that may worsen the situation. Emotionally intelligent project managers can manage their emotions, such as frustration or anxiety, allowing them to think clearly and objectively, even in stressful circumstances.

Empathy and Team Cohesion

A crucial aspect of managing stress in a project environment involves understanding the emotions and concerns of team members. Project managers who exhibit empathy can support and motivate team members facing pressure, creating a more cohesive and resilient team. Emotionally intelligent project managers promote open communication by fostering a culture of trust and compassion, leading to earlier detection and resolution of potential stressors.

Effective Communication

Emotional intelligence enhances communication skills, which are critical for managing effectively managing stress. Clear, empathetic, and transparent communication helps project managers keep their teams informed about project progress, changes, and challenges. Transparent communication reduces uncertainty and anxiety among team members, reducing stress and fostering a positive work environment.

Conflict Resolution

Project managers often encounter conflicts within teams or with stakeholders, which can escalate stress levels. Emotional intelligence equips project managers with the ability to handle conflicts in a constructive manner. They can navigate disagreements, address concerns, and find solutions satisfying all parties involved. This prevents unresolved conflicts from becoming long-term stressors.

Building Resilience

Resilience is the capacity to bounce back from setbacks and challenges. Emotional intelligence strengthens project managers' resilience by helping them reframe negative situations positively. They can view setbacks as learning opportunities and adapt their approach accordingly, reducing the impact of stress on their emotional well-being.

Change Management

In the dynamic landscape of project management, change is an ever-present force that can disrupt plans, challenge team dynamics, and alter project outcomes. Project managers must have the right skills to respond to change and steer their teams through uncertainty effectively. One such indispensable skill is Emotional Intelligence.

This section discusses the profound impact of Emotional Intelligence on project managers' ability to respond to change adeptly.

Practical Applications of Emotional Intelligence in Responding to Change

Recognizing the Need for Change

Emotionally intelligent project managers can detect early signs that change is necessary for project success. These managers can identify potential roadblocks and emerging issues by continuously monitoring project progress and team dynamics. They are more receptive to feedback from team members and stakeholders, which allows them to make timely adjustments to project plans and strategies, fostering adaptability and agility in the face of change.

Leading with Empathy and Understanding

During periods of change, emotions can run high among team members. Emotionally intelligent project managers take the time to understand individual views and anxieties. They actively listen, acknowledging the emotions and challenges team members may experience due to the changes. By demonstrating empathy and support, project managers can alleviate anxiety and resistance, creating a culture of trust and cooperation.

Communicating Change Effectively

Change communication is a critical aspect of project management. Emotionally intelligent project managers carefully plan and execute their communication strategies, considering the needs and preferences of different stakeholders. They use clear and transparent language, avoiding ambiguity and confusion. Regular and open communication channels help keep the team informed, reducing uncertainty and ensuring everyone is aligned throughout the change process.

Building Resilience within the Team

Emotional intelligence enables project managers to nurture resilience within their teams. Resiliency is the ability to bounce back from setbacks and continue forward despite challenges. Emotionally intelligent leaders frame change as an opportunity for growth and learning, empowering team members to embrace change positively. They celebrate successes, acknowledge efforts, and provide support when setbacks occur, fostering a culture of continuous improvement.

Facilitating Collaboration and Innovation

Change often requires creative problem-solving and innovative approaches. Emotionally intelligent project managers encourage collaboration and create an environment where team members feel safe to share ideas and perspectives. By embracing diversity and leveraging the team's collective intelligence, they can devise innovative solutions to navigate change successfully.

Adapting Leadership Styles

Effective project managers adapt their leadership styles to suit the demands of the situation. Some team members may need more guidance and direction during change, while others may thrive with greater autonomy. Emotionally intelligent project managers assess the needs and capabilities of their team members and adjust their leadership styles accordingly, ensuring the team remains engaged and motivated during times of change.

Team Benefits

Emotional Intelligence does not just bring benefits for the individual. Emotional intelligence is equally crucial to the dynamics of a team. This section will discuss the benefits of high emotional intelligence for teams and how it fosters a positive and productive environment, leading to increased trust, performance, and reduced turnover.

1. Creating a Safe Place to Share Ideas

Teams with high emotional intelligence are likelier to cultivate a safe and inclusive atmosphere where every member feels valued and respected. Such an environment encourages individuals to express their ideas without the worry of ridicule or rejection. When team members are comfortable sharing their thoughts openly, it fosters creativity and innovation. By embracing different views and engaging in constructive discussions, teams can find more effective solutions to complex problems.

An emotionally intelligent team leader is pivotal in nurturing this safe space. They demonstrate empathy, active listening, and open communication, encouraging others to follow suit. Consequently, team members feel appreciated and understood, boosting their confidence and willingness to share their unique insights.

2. Building Higher Trust

Trust is the foundation of any high-performing and successful team. High emotional intelligence enhances trust-building among team members by encouraging open dialogue, mutual respect, and vulnerability. Emotional intelligence enables individuals to perceive and understand the emotions of others accurately. When team members sense that their emotions are acknowledged and respected, it fosters a sense of trust and strengthens interpersonal relationships.

Team leaders with high emotional intelligence are adept at building trust among team members by being authentic, consistent, and supportive. They promptly address conflicts, promote transparent communication, and ensure team members feel heard and appreciated. In turn, trust flourishes, and team cohesion and collaboration improve significantly.

3. Less Oversight, Greater Autonomy

Teams with high emotional intelligence can function more independently and require less micro-management. When team members possess emotional intelligence, they are better equipped to manage their emotions, handle stress, and make solid decisions, even in the most challenging situations. This reduces the need for constant oversight, as individuals are empowered to have responsibility for their tasks and contributions.

Leaders in emotionally intelligent teams delegate responsibilities effectively, recognizing the strengths, weaknesses, and expertise areas of each team member. They provide counsel and support when needed, letting team members take ownership of their work. This increased autonomy not only boosts individual confidence and job satisfaction but also enables the team to achieve higher levels of productivity and efficiency.

4. Higher Performance Levels

The benefits of emotional intelligence on team performance are evident in various aspects. Emotionally intelligent teams demonstrate stronger cooperation, effective communication, and better conflict resolution, resulting in streamlined workflows and improved decision-making.

Members of such teams are more attuned to each other's needs and strengths, fostering a collaborative environment where individual talents are harnessed to achieve collective goals. Emotionally intelligent team members are also more likely to offer and receive constructive feedback gracefully, which promotes continuous learning and personal development.

Furthermore, emotionally intelligent team leaders can create a clear and inspiring vision for the team, motivating everyone to work toward shared objectives. They can instill a sense of purpose and meaning in their team, which drives intrinsic motivation and commitment to excellence.

5. Reduced Turnover Rates

High emotional intelligence can have a significant impact on minimizing employee turnover within a team. When team members feel a high sense of value, respect, and support, they are more likely to remain active and committed to the team's goals and objectives.

Emotionally intelligent leaders are attentive to team members' issues and concerns. They actively work to address any issues or challenges that arise and promote a positive work environment that emphasizes work-life balance, growth opportunities, and a sense of belonging.

As a result, team members experience higher job satisfaction and are less likely to seek other opportunities. This reduced turnover saves time and resources on recruitment and training and enhances team stability and continuity, leading to increased productivity and better overall team performance.

High emotional intelligence is a potent force that transforms teams into thriving, efficient, and harmonious units. By fostering a safe space for sharing ideas, building trust, allowing greater autonomy, boosting performance levels, and reducing turnover rates, emotional intelligence creates an environment where each team member can thrive and contribute their best.

Conflict Resolution

Conflict can occur at any time during a project's life cycle. As a project manager, effectively dealing with and resolving conflicts is crucial for ensuring the project's success and maintaining a productive team environment. While technical expertise and strategic planning are essential for managing projects, emotional intelligence plays a pivotal role in navigating the complexities of conflict resolution. This section explores the benefits of high emotional intelligence for project managers and how it fosters effective conflict resolution.

Enhancing Communication and Active Listening

Conflicts often arise due to misunderstandings between parties or miscommunications. Project managers with high emotional intelligence excel in promoting open and honest communication between all team members. They actively listen to concerns, ideas, and feedback, creating an environment where everyone feels heard and valued. This prevents conflicts from escalating and encourages a culture of collaboration and respect throughout the team.

Developing Empathy and Understanding

Empathy is a cornerstone of emotional intelligence. A project manager who can put themselves in others' shoes can better comprehend the underlying emotions driving conflicts. By understanding the needs and concerns of each party involved, they can address the root causes of the conflict rather than merely treating its symptoms. This enables them to find solutions that are fair and considerate of everyone's perspectives.

Managing Stress and Remaining Calm

Project managers often face high-pressure and demanding situations with tight deadlines, leading to stress and tension within the team. A project manager with high emotional intelligence can remain composed even in stressful circumstances. Their ability to manage their emotions prevents them from reacting impulsively or defensively during conflicts. Instead, they respond thoughtfully, rationally, and respectfully, setting a positive example for the team.

Building Trust and Positive Relationships

Trust is essential in any team setting, and project managers play a vital role in fostering trust among team members. High emotional intelligence enables project managers to build strong, positive relationships with their teams by being transparent, approachable, and reliable. When conflicts arise, team members are more likely to trust a project manager with high emotional intelligence to handle the situation fairly and considerately, encouraging cooperation and collaboration.

Encouraging Constructive Conflict

Not all conflicts are harmful; some can be constructive, leading to better outcomes. Project managers with high emotional intelligence can differentiate between destructive conflicts and healthy disagreements. They recognize the value of different perspectives and encourage healthy debate, which can lead to innovative solutions and improved project outcomes.

Effective Mediation and Conflict Resolution

When conflicts arise, a project manager with high emotional intelligence is well-equipped to mediate and resolve them effectively. They can facilitate open discussions, create a safe space for expressing emotions, and guide the parties involved toward finding mutually beneficial resolutions. Their ability to remain neutral and empathetic during the process encourages collaboration and compromise, ultimately leading to satisfactory outcomes for all parties.

Retaining and Motivating Team Members

Conflict within a team can lead to dissatisfaction and demotivation among team members. A project manager with high emotional intelligence can readily spot signs of discontent and address the underlying issues promptly. By fostering a positive team environment through effective conflict resolution, they can retain talented team members and keep them motivated to perform at their best.

Emotional intelligence is a powerful tool in a project manager's arsenal. It enhances team communication, understanding, and trust and enables effective conflict resolution. Project managers with high EI can navigate challenging situations with empathy and composure, fostering a positive team dynamic and ultimately contributing to the project's success. As conflict resolution is an ongoing process in any project, developing and honing emotional intelligence should be a priority for all project managers seeking to excel in their roles.

Benefits/Customer Satisfaction

In project management, success isn't solely determined by completing tasks and meeting deadlines. The true mark of a skilled project manager lies in their ability to understand and connect with people, particularly customers. This is where your emotional intelligence superpower comes into play. In this chapter, we will explore the profound impact of high emotional intelligence on customer satisfaction and how project managers can leverage it to create lasting, positive relationships with their clients.

Understanding the Role of Emotional Intelligence in Customer Satisfaction

Project managers deal with a diverse range of stakeholders daily. From team members and executives to vendors and customers, they must navigate through various personalities, each with unique needs and expectations. The ability to empathize and grasp the emotions driving these stakeholders' actions and decisions is what sets an emotionally intelligent project manager apart.

High emotional intelligence enables project managers to perceive subtle verbal and non-verbal communication cues, allowing them to understand their customers' underlying motivations better. It provides them with the tools to adapt their approach and communication style to match different clients' preferences and emotional states, ultimately leading to improved customer satisfaction.

The Empathy Advantage

Empathy is at the core of emotional intelligence, and it is a vital skill for project managers seeking to foster strong relationships with their customers. By putting themselves in their customers' shoes, project managers can better grasp their needs and concerns, even those that must be addressed. This level of understanding allows them to provide personalized solutions, increasing the likelihood of meeting or exceeding customer expectations.

When customers feel heard and understood, they are more likely to trust the project manager and the team's abilities. This trust forms the foundation of a positive and long-lasting relationship, reducing the risk of misunderstandings or conflicts and ultimately leading to higher customer satisfaction.

Emotional Regulation and Conflict Resolution

Projects are not immune to challenges, and conflicts with customers may arise. In these situations, a project manager with high emotional intelligence can be a potent mediator. They can keep their emotions in check, even in tense situations, and maintain a calm and composed demeanor. Doing so creates an atmosphere of respect and open communication, making it easier to find mutually agreeable resolutions.

Emotionally intelligent project managers also understand the importance of managing their teams' emotions during stress or conflict. By fostering a positive team culture and providing emotional support, they ensure that team members can work cohesively, even in challenging circumstances. This, in turn, reflects positively on the project's outcomes and customer satisfaction.

Recognizing and Leveraging Customer Feedback

Customer feedback is a treasure trove of valuable insights. Emotionally intelligent project managers approach feedback with an open mind and without becoming defensive. They recognize that feedback, even if critical, is an opportunity for growth and improvement.

When customers provide feedback, an emotionally intelligent project manager listens actively, seeking to understand the underlying emotions behind the comments. They know that emotions often drive feedback, and addressing those emotions can lead to more meaningful solutions.

Moreover, emotionally intelligent project managers involve their customers in the problem-solving process. They appreciate the feedback and collaborate with customers to find mutually beneficial solutions. This approach enhances customer satisfaction and reinforces the project manager's reputation as someone who genuinely cares about their clients.

Building Lasting Relationships

Project managers with high emotional intelligence have a unique advantage in building lasting customer relationships. They go beyond the boundaries of a single project and focus on the bigger picture— the long-term relationship with the customer. They invest time and effort in nurturing the bond, ensuring that customers feel valued and supported throughout their journey with the organization.

The emotional connection established by an emotionally intelligent project manager strengthens the customer's loyalty to the organization. Happy customers are more likely to become repeat customers, providing valuable referrals and testimonials contributing to the organization's overall success.

Emotional intelligence is a powerful asset for project managers seeking customer satisfaction. By understanding the emotions of their customers and responding with empathy and professionalism, project managers can forge strong relationships, handle conflicts effectively, and leverage customer feedback to improve their services continuously.

As organizations increasingly recognize the significance of emotional intelligence in project management, cultivating this skill becomes a crucial aspect of professional development for project managers. By embracing emotional intelligence, project managers can elevate their performance, increase customer satisfaction, and position themselves as invaluable assets to their organizations in a competitive and ever-evolving business landscape.

Influence

In project management, success often hinges on influencing and persuading stakeholders effectively. Project managers with a higher level of influence can navigate challenges with greater ease, foster collaboration, and secure the necessary support to complete projects successfully. This section explores the benefits of project managers with high emotional intelligence and how it translates into high levels of influence in various contexts.

The Influence with Customers

When project managers possess high emotional intelligence, they can establish a deeper connection with customers, leading to various advantages:

- **Building Trust:** High emotional intelligence enables project managers to be empathetic, actively listening to customers' needs and concerns. This fosters trust, strengthening rapport and long-term relationships, as clients feel heard and understood.

- **Effective Communication:** Emotionally intelligent project managers can communicate complex ideas clearly, using language that resonates with the customer. This skill facilitates better project comprehension and ensures alignment with customer expectations.

- **Conflict Resolution:** No project is free from challenges, and conflicts with customers may arise. Project managers with high emotional intelligence are adept at handling disputes gracefully, addressing concerns with empathy, and finding mutually beneficial solutions.

- **Managing Expectations:** Emotionally intelligent project managers set realistic customer expectations, avoiding overpromising and underdelivering. Clear communication of project scope and potential limitations establishes transparency and credibility.

- **Customer Loyalty:** Satisfied and emotionally connected customers become loyal advocates, recommending the project manager and the organization to others. Positive word-of-mouth can significantly impact the company's reputation and create new opportunities.

The Influence within the Organization

Apart from fostering more robust customer relationships, project managers with high emotional intelligence can exert considerable influence within their organization:

- **Team Cohesion:** EI enables project managers to understand their team members' strengths, weaknesses, and motivations. By leveraging this knowledge, they can build cohesive teams, assigning tasks that play to individual strengths and fostering a sense of camaraderie.

- **Conflict Management:** In any organization, conflicts are bound to occur. Emotionally intelligent project managers are skilled at managing conflicts among team members, finding common ground, and promoting a harmonious work environment.

- **Inspirational Leadership:** High emotional intelligence allows project managers to lead by example, displaying a positive attitude and motivating their teams to perform at their best. Inspirational leadership boosts morale, productivity, and team loyalty.

- **Negotiation and Influence:** Project managers must often negotiate with stakeholders, senior management, or other departments to secure additional resources or funding. Emotional intelligence empowers them to be persuasive, understand the concerns and needs of others, and make a compelling case for their projects.

- **Adaptability and Resilience:** Emotionally intelligent project managers cope better with change and uncertainty. They adapt quickly to unforeseen challenges, keeping their teams focused and resilient during turbulent times.

Gaining Management Attention and Resources

Project managers with high emotional intelligence are better positioned to gain management attention and secure additional resources or funding for their projects:

- **Effective Communication:** Emotional Intelligence helps project managers articulate their project's value proposition and potential benefits to the organization. Clear, concise, and persuasive communication will likely capture management's attention and support.

- **Building Relationships with Stakeholders:** Emotionally intelligent project managers invest time and effort in nurturing relationships with key stakeholders. These strong connections increase the likelihood of gaining influential supporters who can champion their cause at higher levels of the organization.

- **Presenting with Impact:** When project managers possess high emotional Intelligence, they are more adept at gauging the mood and receptiveness of their audience. This insight allows them to tailor their presentations to resonate with decision-makers, increasing the chances of obtaining approval and resources.

- **Creating a Positive Reputation:** Project managers with high emotional intelligence build a positive reputation as influential leaders who prioritize team well-being and successful project delivery. A positive track record enhances their credibility and increases their influence in decision-making processes.

- **Adopting a Strategic Mindset:** High EI enables project managers to think strategically, aligning their projects with the organization's goals and objectives. By demonstrating how their projects contribute to the company's success, they gain support from management and access to more resources.

Emotional intelligence is a game-changer in project management. Project managers who possess high emotional intelligence build stronger relationships with customers and wield significant influence within their organizations. By leveraging empathy, effective communication, and relationship-building skills, emotionally intelligent project managers gain management attention, secure additional resources, and lead their teams to achieve exceptional outcomes. As the business landscape evolves, emotional intelligence becomes an indispensable asset for project managers seeking to thrive and make a lasting impact on their projects and organizations.

Enhancing the Superpower: Tools for Project Managers to Excel Emotionally

In the dynamic world of project management, project managers are often seen as the people that get things done. They bring order to chaos, deliver results against all odds, and lead diverse teams toward a common goal. Yet, behind the impressive façade of their organizational prowess lies a crucial but often overlooked aspect of their effectiveness: emotional intelligence. Emotions, the subtle undercurrents that shape human interactions, are the true superpower that sets exceptional project managers apart from the rest. This book chapter will explore different tools project managers can use to manage and increase their emotional intelligence prowess.

Think of these tools like a Swiss army knife. The Swiss Army knife has many blades, each designed for a specific purpose- from cutting and sawing to opening cans and bottles. In the same way, our emotional intelligence toolkit comprises a variety of instruments, each tailored to address particular emotional challenges that project managers may encounter.

Let's go over some of these tools.

Journaling

Journaling is a practice that empowers project managers to gain insights into their emotions, thought patterns, and behaviors. When done consistently, journaling can lead to increased self-awareness and emotional regulation.

What is Journaling? Journaling involves the practice of writing down thoughts, experiences, and reflections regularly. Journaling allows for a safe space for self-expression, allowing project managers to explore their feelings, concerns, and successes in a structured manner. Journaling is a personal and private activity that encourages individuals to be open and honest with themselves.

Techniques for Journaling to Increase Emotional Intelligence

There are various journaling techniques that project managers can employ to enhance their emotional intelligence:

Daily Reflections: Allocate time each day for reflective journaling, wherein project managers can analyze their emotional experiences and reactions during the day's interactions. This helps them identify patterns and triggers that may influence their behavior.

Gratitude Journaling: Expressing gratitude in a journal can foster a positive outlook and promote emotional well-being. Project managers can write about what they are grateful for in their professional and personal lives.

Emotional Release Journaling: This technique involves venting emotions constructively through writing. When facing challenging situations or conflicts, project managers can use their journals to release pent-up emotions and gain clarity.

Future-Self Journaling: Project managers can envision their ideal future selves in their journals. By writing about their aspirations, goals, and emotional strengths, they can create a clear path for self-improvement.

Brainstorming Solutions: When confronted with complex problems, journaling can be used as a brainstorming tool to explore potential solutions and evaluate the emotional implications of each option.

Topics to Journal About for Increased Emotional Intelligence

Project managers can journal about many different topics to enhance their emotional intelligence. By delving into these subjects, project managers gain deeper insights into their emotions and thought processes.

Self-Reflections: Journaling to explore their emotions, identifying both positive and negative feelings they experience during the day and the events that triggered these emotions.

Communication and Interpersonal Dynamics: Journaling about challenging interactions with team members, stakeholders, or clients allows project managers to assess their communication styles and emotional responses.

Handling Stress and Pressure: Project managers often face high-pressure situations. Journaling about their stress triggers and coping mechanisms can lead to better stress management.

Decision-Making: Explore the emotional factors influencing decision-making processes, including biases, fears, and desires, to make more balanced choices.

Goal Progression: Regularly documenting progress towards personal and professional goals helps project managers stay motivated and provides insight into emotional patterns associated with goal achievement.

Utilizing the Journal to Enhance Emotional Intelligence

This section focuses on how project managers can use their journals effectively to boost their emotional intelligence and improve their project management skills.

Recognizing Emotional Patterns: Regularly reviewing past journal entries allows project managers to identify recurring emotional patterns and triggers. With awareness, they can work towards healthier responses.

Building Emotional Vocabulary: By consistently describing their emotions in their journals, project managers expand their emotional vocabulary, improving communication and empathy with others.

Emotional Regulation and Stress Management: Journaling about stressful situations provides project managers with insights into their stressors, enabling them to develop coping strategies and emotional regulation techniques.

Enhancing Empathy and Understanding Others: Encourage project managers to reflect on the emotions of team members and stakeholders they interact with, helping them develop a deeper sense of empathy and understanding.

Gaining Clarity and Problem-Solving: Journaling can serve as a problem-solving tool, enabling project managers to explore alternative perspectives and identify the best course of action.

Journaling is a powerful tool for project managers seeking to enhance their emotional intelligence and, consequently, their project management effectiveness. By engaging in regular and introspective journaling practices, project managers can better understand their emotions, thoughts, and behaviors, leading to increased self-awareness, empathy, and emotional regulation. Integrating emotional intelligence into project management practices creates a more positive and productive work environment, ultimately fostering project success and personal growth for project managers.

Meditation

Meditation is a practice that has been around for centuries. It involves training the brain to achieve a state of heightened awareness and focus. Numerous studies have proven its positive effects on emotional intelligence, making it an invaluable tool for project managers. Here are some of the key benefits:

✓ **Enhanced Self-Awareness:** Meditation allows project managers to become more focused on their mental awareness, emotions, and reactions. Through regular practice, they can identify behavior patterns and triggers, enabling them to respond thoughtfully rather than impulsively.

✓ **Stress Reduction:** The high-stress nature of project management can lead to personal burnout and lower productivity. Meditation helps project managers develop resilience and manage stress more effectively, allowing them to stay composed and focused during challenging times.

✓ **Improved Decision-Making:** Clarity of mind gained through meditation leads to better decision-making. Project managers can weigh options more objectively, considering the needs of stakeholders and the project team, leading to more balanced and well-informed choices.

✓ **Empathy and Understanding**: Meditation cultivates empathy by encouraging a non-judgmental attitude towards yourself and as well as others. This creates a state of understanding and compassion within the project team, improving collaboration and team dynamics.

✓ **Conflict Resolution:** With increased emotional intelligence, project managers can handle conflicts more purposefully and tactfully. They can actively listen, validate feelings, and find common ground for resolving issues, promoting a harmonious work environment.

Techniques for Project Managers New to Meditation

For project managers unfamiliar with meditation, starting a practice may seem daunting. However, incorporating meditation into one's routine can be simple and highly effective. Here are some techniques to get started:

Mindful Breathing: Perhaps the easiest way to begin meditation is by focusing on the breath. Find a quiet place, sit in a comfortable position, and close your eyes. Take slow, deep breaths, and feel how your breath enters and leaves the body. If your mind starts to drift, gently focus your thoughts back on your breathing. Start with just 5 minutes and slowly increase the duration over time.

Guided Meditations: Many mobile apps and websites offer guided meditation sessions. These are especially helpful for beginners as they provide expert instructions and help maintain focus. Choose sessions that target emotional intelligence, self-awareness, or stress reduction.

Body Scan: The body scan is a technique that promotes relaxation and body awareness. Begin by lying down or sitting comfortably. Close your eyes and bring your attention to different body parts, starting from the toes and gradually moving to the head. Notice any tension or sensations without judgment and allow them to release.

Loving-Kindness Meditation: This meditation cultivates compassion and empathy towards oneself and others. While sitting quietly, repeat phrases such as "May I be happy, may I be healthy, may I be safe" or customize them for specific individuals. Extend these wishes to colleagues, team members, and project stakeholders.

Walking Meditation: Meditation doesn't always have to be done in a sitting down stationary position. Walking meditation involves being present and mindful while walking slowly and deliberately. Pay attention to the sensation of every step, how the body moves, and the environment which is present around you.

As a project manager, developing emotional intelligence is a valuable investment that leads to more successful projects, happier teams, and personal growth. Meditation is a practical and accessible tool to enhance emotional intelligence and can be integrated into even the busiest schedules. By dedicating just a few minutes each day to meditation, project managers can harness the power of self-awareness, empathy, and stress reduction, ultimately empowering their projects through emotional intelligence. So, take a deep breath, find a quiet moment, and begin your journey toward becoming an emotionally intelligent project manager. The positive impact will extend far beyond the projects you lead, benefiting both your professional and personal life.

Practicing Gratitude

Practicing gratitude as a project manager entails actively acknowledging and expressing genuine appreciation for team members' and stakeholders' efforts, dedication, and contributions throughout the project lifecycle. It involves recognizing the hard work and achievements of the team, even during challenging times, and valuing the unique skills and perspectives that each individual brings to the project. A grateful project manager creates a positive and supportive work environment where team members feel valued and motivated to excel. By regularly expressing gratitude and recognizing the team's successes, a project manager fosters a culture of appreciation, collaboration, and trust, improving team morale, enhanced communication, and, ultimately, a more successful and empowered project.

Benefits of Practicing Gratitude and Emotional Intelligence:

✓ **Enhancing Team Morale and Motivation:** When project managers express genuine appreciation for their team members' efforts, it fosters a positive and supportive work environment. Gratitude creates a sense of value and recognition, boosting team members' morale and motivation to excel in their roles. Recognizing team members' contributions can increase job satisfaction and reduce the risk of burnout, promoting long-term commitment to the project's success.

✓ **Strengthening Interpersonal Relationships:** Emotional intelligence is a vital aspect of successful project management, as it enables managers to understand and connect with team members in a more understanding way. By being emotionally intelligent, project managers can empathize with their team, build trust, and handle conflicts with more remarkable finesse. The practice of gratitude plays a crucial role in building strong interpersonal relationships, as expressing gratitude cultivates a sense of trust and camaraderie among team members.

✓ **Improving Communication and Collaboration:** Project success heavily relies on effective communication and collaboration. Gratitude enhances communication by fostering an open and appreciative atmosphere where team members feel comfortable sharing ideas and concerns. Emotional intelligence allows project managers to interpret non-verbal cues and adapt their communication styles to suit the needs of individual team members, promoting a more inclusive and productive work environment.

✓ **Boosting Resilience and Problem-Solving:** Projects are not without challenges, and emotional intelligence, coupled with gratitude, can help project managers and teams navigate difficult times with resilience. Gratitude enables individuals to focus on the positive aspects even during challenging situations, reducing stress and facilitating creative problem-solving. Emotionally intelligent project managers can inspire their teams to adopt a solution-oriented mindset by acknowledging their resilience and dedication to overcoming obstacles.

Practical Ways to Practice Gratitude as a Project Manager:

Expressing Verbal Appreciation: Simple acts of expressing gratitude through verbal appreciation can go a long way in motivating and empowering team members. Whether in team meetings or one-on-one conversations, project managers should take the time to recognize and thank individuals for their contributions and accomplishments. A heartfelt "thank you" can significantly boost team morale and reinforce positive behavior.

Providing Recognition and Rewards: A formal recognition and reward system within the project management framework can foster a culture of appreciation. Acknowledging exceptional performance publicly through team-wide announcements or during project reviews makes the recognized team member feel valued and inspires others to excel.

Creating a Gratitude Journal: Encourage team members to maintain a gratitude journal where they can write down things they are grateful for on a daily or weekly basis. As a project manager, you can lead by example and share your gratitude reflections regularly. This practice promotes self-awareness and helps individuals focus on the positives amidst the challenges they may encounter during the project.

Practicing Active Listening: Emotionally intelligent project managers actively listen to their team members' concerns, feedback, and ideas. Demonstrating attentive listening and validating their perspectives fosters trust and promotes open communication. When team members feel heard and understood, they are more likely to be engaged and committed to the project's success.

Celebrating Milestones and Achievements: As the project progresses, celebrate milestones and achievements to recognize the team's collective efforts. Organize small celebrations or team-building activities to commemorate critical project phases or successful project completions. Such events allow team members to bond and feel a sense of pride in their efforts.

Gratitude is a powerful tool that can elevate the effectiveness of project managers and empower project teams. Project managers can create a positive and motivated workforce by fostering a culture of appreciation and recognizing the importance of emotional intelligence. The benefits of practicing gratitude in project management extend beyond project success, as they contribute to team members' overall well-being and satisfaction. Embracing emotional intelligence and gratitude is about managing projects and nurturing a thriving and collaborative project environment that paves the way for continued success and growth.

Seek Social Support

Social support refers to the network of individuals who offer emotional, practical, or assistance. In emotional intelligence, seeking social support involves reaching out to trusted friends, mentors, and colleagues for guidance, empathy, and constructive feedback. Through these interpersonal connections, individuals can bolster their emotional intelligence and navigate project management challenges with greater confidence and resilience.

Emotional Feedback and Self-awareness

Friends and co-workers play a pivotal role in providing emotional feedback, which is essential for developing self-awareness—a fundamental aspect of emotional intelligence. They offer valuable insights into our emotional patterns, reactions, and blind spots. By encouraging open and honest conversations, these trusted allies can help project managers identify areas for improvement, enabling them to gain a deeper understanding of their emotions and reactions in various situations.

A supportive environment cultivated by friends and colleagues fosters a safe space for introspection and self-reflection. As project managers become more attuned to their emotions and reactions, they can better gauge their strengths, weaknesses, and emotional triggers, leading to increased self-awareness and, consequently, higher emotional intelligence.

Empathy and Social Awareness

Empathy, the ability to recognize and share the feelings of others, is a foundational component of emotional intelligence. Friends and co-workers can act as empathetic sounding boards, offering different perspectives and experiences. Through active listening and genuine concern, they help project managers develop a stronger sense of social awareness.

By interacting with diverse individuals, project managers gain exposure to a broad spectrum of emotions, allowing them to recognize and empathize with the feelings of others more readily. This heightened empathy equips project managers with the tools to create a more empathetic and inclusive work environment, fostering better collaboration and robust team dynamics.

Coping Mechanisms and Emotional Regulation

Projects often come with challenges, setbacks, and high-pressure situations that can trigger emotional responses. Friends and co-workers can provide valuable support by sharing their coping mechanisms and strategies for emotional regulation. Observing how others manage stress, conflicts, and complicated emotions can be an invaluable learning experience for project managers.

Regularly interacting with emotionally intelligent individuals can help project managers develop healthier coping mechanisms, such as mindfulness practices, emotional self-regulation, and adaptive problem-solving. These coping strategies increase emotional resilience, allowing project managers to navigate challenging situations more effectively and bounce back from setbacks with renewed determination.

Influence of Social Circles on Emotional Intelligence

Our emotions and behaviors are heavily influenced by the people we spend the most time with. If project managers surround themselves with emotionally intelligent individuals, they are more likely to adopt and internalize similar emotional intelligence skills and attributes. Positive emotions and constructive ways of dealing with challenges become the norm within such circles, reinforcing and fostering emotional intelligence among all members.

Conversely, a toxic or unsupportive social environment can hinder emotional intelligence growth, perpetuating negative patterns and impeding personal development. Project managers must be intentional about the relationships they cultivate to ensure they are aligning themselves with individuals who promote emotional intelligence.

Emotional Contagion and Team Dynamics

Emotional contagion is when one person's emotions and related behaviors spread to others nearby. In project management, where teamwork is pivotal, emotional contagion can significantly impact team dynamics and project outcomes. When project managers exhibit emotional intelligence, it positively influences their team members, leading to better collaboration, communication, and overall project performance.

Seeking social support from friends and co-workers can be a potent catalyst for enhancing emotional intelligence in project managers. Providing emotional feedback, empathy, coping strategies, and a supportive environment, these social connections aid in developing self-awareness, social awareness, and emotional regulation.

Additionally, the influential role of social circles reinforces the importance of intentionally surrounding oneself with emotionally intelligent individuals to foster personal and professional growth.

As project managers strive to become more emotionally intelligent, they must recognize the significance of cultivating positive and supportive relationships. By empowering themselves through social support, project managers can create a ripple effect of emotional intelligence, positively impacting their teams, projects, and overall success in project management.

Physical Exercise

Physical exercise has been scientifically proven to positively impact various aspects of human well-being, including mental and emotional health. The connection between physical activity and emotional intelligence lies in the influence exercise has on brain chemistry and neural pathways. Regular exercise triggers the release of neurotransmitters, such as endorphins, dopamine, and serotonin, which play vital roles in regulating mood, reducing stress, and overall emotional health.

Stress Reduction

Stress is a natural response to challenging environments. However, it can lead to burnout and decreased emotional intelligence if not managed properly. Engaging in physical exercise helps to alleviate stress by reducing cortisol levels, the hormone responsible for the body's stress response. When project managers integrate regular exercise into their routines, they can effectively manage stress, remain cool and calm under pressure, and make better decisions.

Enhanced Self-awareness

Self-awareness is the foundation of emotional intelligence, which involves understanding one's emotions, strengths, weaknesses, and triggers. Physical exercise provides an opportunity for introspection, allowing project managers to tune into their feelings and thoughts during their workout sessions. Whether going for a mindful walk or engaging in yoga, exercise can be a time for self-reflection, leading to increased self-awareness and a better understanding of emotional patterns.

Improved Mood and Positivity

Emotions are contagious, and as project leaders, project managers have a considerable impact on their team's morale. Regular physical exercise releases endorphins, often called "feel-good" hormones, which promote a positive frame of mind. When project managers approach their work positively and upbeat, it can inspire and motivate their teams, leading to improved collaboration and higher productivity.

Empathy and Relationship Building

Emotional intelligence encompasses empathizing with others, understanding their emotions, and building meaningful relationships. Physical exercise can foster empathy in project managers by encouraging teamwork and social interactions in group activities or fitness classes. Engaging in exercise with colleagues or team members can create a sense of camaraderie, mutual support, and trust, enhancing the emotional bond among team members.

Resilience and Adaptability

Project managers often encounter setbacks, challenges, and unexpected changes throughout the project lifecycle. Building emotional resilience and adaptability is crucial for navigating such situations effectively. Regular physical exercise helps individuals develop mental toughness, enabling them to bounce back from setbacks and remain flexible in the face of change. The discipline required to maintain a consistent exercise routine translates to a project manager's ability to persevere and adapt in challenging project circumstances.

Stress Coping Mechanisms

When faced with high-stress situations, individuals with high emotional intelligence can employ healthy coping mechanisms to maintain their composure and focus. Physical exercise is a positive outlet for stress, replacing potentially harmful coping strategies such as excessive caffeine consumption or emotional eating. Regular exercise empowers project managers to manage stress effectively, leading to better decision-making and a healthier work-life balance.

Mindfulness and Emotional Regulation

Mindfulness, the practice of being fully present and non-judgmental of one's thoughts and emotions, is a crucial aspect of emotional intelligence. Various physical activities, such as yoga and tai chi, incorporate mindfulness techniques. These practices encourage project managers to be in the moment, acknowledge their emotions, and develop emotional regulation skills. The ability to respond thoughtfully rather than impulsively is a hallmark of emotionally intelligent project managers.

Incorporating physical exercise into the lives of project managers can be a transformative approach to developing emotional intelligence. As they care for their physical health, they simultaneously strengthen their emotional well-being, becoming more adept at understanding and managing their emotions and those of their team members. By reducing stress, enhancing self-awareness, promoting empathy, and fostering resilience, exercise empowers project managers to effectively lead their teams with emotional intelligence. Embracing physical activity as a tool for emotional intelligence will undoubtedly lead to more successful, harmonious, and empowered projects in the ever-challenging world of project management.

Cognitive Reframing

Cognitive reframing is a mind-altering technique that consciously changes how we interpret and perceive events or situations. It enables project managers to shift from negative or unproductive thought patterns to positive and constructive views. By practicing cognitive reframing, project managers can gain greater control over their emotional responses and, in turn, positively impact their decision-making and leadership capabilities.

Identifying Limiting Beliefs

Limiting beliefs are deep-rooted negative thoughts or assumptions people have about themselves, others, or the ecosystem around them. These beliefs act as mental barriers, restricting personal growth and potential. Often formed through past experiences, upbringing, or societal conditioning, limiting beliefs can hinder individuals from taking risks, pursuing opportunities, or reaching their full potential. They often manifest as self-doubt, fear of failure, or feelings of inadequacy, preventing individuals from embracing new challenges or stepping outside their comfort zones. Identifying and challenging these limiting beliefs is crucial for personal development and growth, as it opens the door to new possibilities and allows individuals to embrace a more positive and empowered outlook on life.

The first step in cognitive reframing is to identify and challenge limiting beliefs. Project managers often face challenging circumstances that trigger negative thoughts, such as "This project is doomed to fail" or "I can't handle this pressure." These limiting beliefs hinder effective decision-making and can lead to self-doubt.

By being aware of these negative thoughts, project managers can start the process of cognitive reframing. They can ask themselves, "Is this belief based on evidence or just my perception?" Questioning these beliefs opens the door to more balanced and constructive interpretations.

Reframing Negative Thoughts

Once limiting beliefs are recognized, project managers can reframe them into more optimistic and empowering thoughts. For instance, instead of thinking, "This project is doomed to fail," they can reframe it as "This project has its challenges, but with a proactive approach, we can overcome them."

Reframing allows project managers to approach problems with a growth mindset, which can lead to better solutions and a more resilient team. It helps them see setbacks as opportunities to learn and grow rather than obstacles that cannot be overcome.

Managing Stress and Pressure

Project managers often face immense stress and pressure from stakeholders, team members, and tight deadlines. Unmanaged stress can lead to emotional reactions that may negatively impact decision-making and relationships.

Through cognitive reframing, project managers can reinterpret stress as a natural part of the job with exciting opportunities for success. Viewing stress as a challenge rather than a threat can help project managers stay composed, think clearly, and maintain focus during turbulent times.

Fostering Effective Communication

Emotional intelligence is intertwined with effective communication. Project managers who practice cognitive reframing are more likely to respond constructively to feedback and criticism. Instead of becoming defensive, they can view feedback as an opportunity for improvement and growth.

Moreover, reframing can enhance how project managers deliver feedback to their teams. Constructive feedback framed positively can inspire team members to perform better, fostering a culture of open communication and continuous improvement.

Building Stronger Teams

Project success relies heavily on the dynamics within the team. Emotionally intelligent project managers who practice cognitive reframing can better understand and empathize with their team members' perspectives, needs, and challenges. This understanding builds trust and encourages team members to openly share their ideas and concerns.

Furthermore, cognitive reframing can help in conflict resolution. Instead of approaching conflicts with defensiveness or aggression, project managers can reframe disputes as opportunities to strengthen relationships and find mutually beneficial solutions.

In the emotionally intelligent project manager's toolkit, cognitive reframing is potent for fostering effective leadership, communication, and team dynamics. By identifying and challenging limiting beliefs, reframing negative thoughts, managing stress, and building stronger teams, project managers can elevate their emotional intelligence and, in turn, empower their projects toward success.

Cognitive reframing is not a quick fix but a skill requiring continuous practice and self-awareness. As project managers embrace this technique, they will find themselves better equipped to handle project management challenges with poise, empathy, and a clear focus on achieving outstanding results. Embracing emotional intelligence through cognitive reframing is a transformative journey that benefits project managers and their teams.

Practicing Empathy

Empathy is the ability to comprehend and understand how other people feel from their point of view. It enables project managers to step into the shoes of team members, stakeholders, and clients, gaining insights into their emotions, thoughts, and concerns. By displaying empathy, project managers validate the experiences of others, showing genuine care and concern, which leads to stronger relationships, trust, and a positive team dynamic.

Benefits of Practicing Empathy in Project Management

Improved Communication: Empathy fosters effective communication, as project managers can discern the emotional context underlying messages and respond appropriately. They listen actively, ask insightful questions, and validate the concerns of their team members. This approach reduces misunderstandings and miscommunications, leading to a more streamlined project workflow.

Enhanced Team Collaboration: A project manager who possesses empathy establishes a secure and nurturing atmosphere, fostering a sense of confidence among team members to express their thoughts and worries freely. By recognizing and appreciating their input, the project manager enhances team spirit, resulting in heightened cooperation and innovation.

Conflict Resolution: Conflicts occur in every project, but empathy can be a game-changing tool for resolution. When conflicts arise, an empathetic project manager listens to all parties, validates their feelings, and seeks common ground. This approach de-escalates tensions and promotes a more constructive atmosphere for resolving issues.

Increased Employee Engagement: Employees who feel heard and understood are likelier to be happier and more engaged in their work. An empathetic project manager shows genuine interest in the well-being and growth of their team members. A natural byproduct of this is team members with high job satisfaction and productivity.

Client and Stakeholder Relations: Empathy is not limited to internal team dynamics but extends to external relationships. Understanding the needs and expectations of clients and stakeholders helps project managers tailor their approach, leading to more successful project outcomes and satisfied clients.

Developing Empathy as a Project Manager

Empathy is a stagnant trait. Empathy is a skill that can be learned and improved over time. Here are some strategies for project managers to develop and practice empathy:

✓ Active Listening: focus on others when they speak, making eye contact and avoiding interruptions. Listen without judgment and try to understand the emotions behind their words.

✓ Perspective-Taking: Put yourself in the other person's position and consider how they feel or think. This exercise can help you see situations from different viewpoints.

✓ Emotional Regulation: Acquire the skill of effectively handling your emotions, enabling you to maintain composure and empathy even when faced with difficult circumstances.

✓ Empathy Training: Some organizations offer training programs focused on developing individual emotional intelligence and empathy. Participating in such programs can provide valuable insights and practical techniques.

✓ Reflective Practice: Reflect on your interactions with team members and stakeholders. Consider how you could have responded with more empathy and use those insights in future interactions.

Emotional intelligence is a critical asset for project managers, and empathy stands at its core. By practicing compassion, project managers can build stronger relationships with their team, clients, and stakeholders, leading to increased collaboration, improved communication, and successful project outcomes. Developing empathy is an ongoing journey, but its transformative impact on project management makes it a skill worth investing time and effort in. As project managers embrace compassion, they empower projects to reach new heights and create an environment where everyone can thrive and excel.

Mindful Eating

Mindful eating is the practice of watching the food we eat, including how it tastes, its texture, and how it makes us feel physically and emotionally. By practicing mindful eating, we become more aware of the relationship between our emotions and food choices, improving emotional intelligence.

Increasing Emotional Intelligence through Nourishing Foods

Certain foods can enhance emotional intelligence by promoting brain health, stabilizing moods, and fostering emotional resilience. Incorporating the following foods into the project manager's diet can significantly contribute to increasing emotional intelligence:

a. Omega-3 Fatty Acids: Foods rich in omega-3 fatty acids, such as fatty fish (salmon, mackerel, and sardines), chia seeds, and walnuts, are linked to improved cognitive function and reduced symptoms of anxiety and depression. As a result, project managers who consume these foods may experience increased emotional resilience and better decision-making under stress.

b. Dark Leafy Greens: Leafy greens like spinach, kale, and Swiss chard are abundant in magnesium, a mineral known to regulate stress hormones and promote a sense of calmness. Project managers who consume dark leafy greens may find it easier to stay composed during challenging project situations.

c. Berries: Blueberries, strawberries, and blackberries are rich in antioxidants that can assist in protecting the brain from oxidative stress. These fruits also contain flavonoids that positively influence cognitive function, potentially enhancing a project manager's ability to understand and manage emotions.

d. Complex Carbohydrates: Foods like whole grains and sweet potatoes provide a steady release of glucose, stabilizing blood sugar levels and promoting emotional stability. As project managers maintain balanced energy levels, they are more likely to approach their teams with patience and empathy.

*Foods that May Decrease Emotional Intelligence

Just as some foods can enhance emotional intelligence, certain dietary choices may hinder emotional well-being and impede effective project management. Project managers should be mindful of the following foods and their potential negative impacts on emotional intelligence:

a. Sugary Snacks and Beverages: Foods high in refined sugars, such as candies, pastries, and sugary drinks, can cause blood sugar to increase drastically and is often followed by hard crashes. These fluctuations can lead to irritability, mood swings, and reduced emotional regulation.

b. <u>Processed Foods</u>: Processed foods often have high levels of unhealthy fats, preservatives, and artificial additives. Consuming these foods regularly may contribute to inflammation and negatively affect brain function, potentially hindering a project manager's ability to stay composed and make thoughtful decisions.

c. <u>Excessive Caffeine</u>: While moderate caffeine intake can boost alertness, excessive consumption may lead to anxiety and restlessness. Project managers should be cautious not to rely heavily on caffeine to cope with stress, which may hinder emotional resilience in the long run.

As project managers aim to empower projects through emotional intelligence, incorporating mindful eating practices becomes valuable. Mindful eating allows project managers to make intentional food choices that nourish their bodies and minds, ultimately enhancing emotional intelligence. Project managers can foster empathy, resilience, and effective decision-making by including foods that increase emotional intelligence, such as those rich in omega-3 fatty acids, dark leafy greens, and berries. Conversely, avoiding foods that may decrease emotional intelligence, such as sugary snacks and excessive caffeine, will help project managers maintain emotional balance and ensure a harmonious work environment. Embracing mindful eating as part of their leadership journey, project managers can truly empower their projects through the power of emotional intelligence.

Stress Management Techniques

Stress is a natural response to the challenging situations project management can bring. But unmanaged stress can lead to emotional upheaval, impairing judgment and communication. Emotional intelligence acts as a buffer against stress, helping project managers to recognize and manage their emotions constructively. By developing emotional intelligence, project managers can become more resilient, adaptable, and capable of handling the pressures of their roles.

Stress Management Techniques:

Mindfulness and Meditation: Mindfulness and meditation are powerful stress management techniques that promote self-awareness and emotional regulation. By engaging in regular mindfulness practices, project managers can learn to be present in the moment, observe their thoughts and emotions without judgment, and bring about a calmer state of mind. Mindfulness enables project managers to make better choices and respond more effectively to stressors.

Example: A project manager, overwhelmed by a sudden budget cut, practices mindfulness to acknowledge their anxiety without reacting impulsively. This allows them to think rationally and explore alternative solutions, such as reallocating resources or seeking external funding, instead of panicking and jeopardizing the project.

Time Management and Prioritization: Time management and prioritization skills are crucial stress management skills for project managers. By organizing tasks, setting realistic deadlines, and focusing on high-priority activities, they can reduce the feeling of being overwhelmed and maintain control over their projects.

Example: A project manager faces multiple project tasks and deadlines simultaneously. Instead of tackling everything individually, they prioritize tasks based on urgency and importance. This approach not only prevents burnout but also allows them to allocate sufficient time to each task, improving the quality of their work.

Emotional Resilience Training: Emotional resilience training equips project managers to bounce back from setbacks and remain composed under pressure. It involves recognizing negative emotions, reframing negative thoughts, and fostering a positive outlook even in challenging circumstances.

Example: When a significant project setback occurs due to unforeseen circumstances, an emotionally resilient project manager acknowledges their disappointment but focuses on finding solutions rather than dwelling on the failure. Maintaining a positive attitude inspires the team to persevere and overcome obstacles together.

Emotional Venting and Support Networks: Encouraging emotional venting and establishing a support network are essential aspects of stress management for project managers. Allowing team members to express their frustrations, concerns, or anxieties fosters a supportive and collaborative work environment.

Example: During a team meeting, a project manager notices signs of stress among team members. They create a safe space for everyone to share their feelings openly. By actively listening and offering support, the project manager demonstrates empathy, fostering trust and cohesion within the team.

Impact on Emotional Intelligence:

As project managers incorporate stress management techniques into their daily routines, they experience a positive shift in their emotional intelligence. Here's how these techniques can enhance specific aspects of emotional intelligence:

Self-Awareness: Stress management practices enable project managers to become more aware of their emotional triggers and reactions. They can proactively address their stressors and prevent emotional outbursts by understanding them.

Self-Regulation: With effective stress management, project managers control their emotions and responses better. They can resist impulsive reactions and make more thoughtful decisions, even in high-pressure situations.

Empathy: By managing their stress, project managers become more attuned to the emotional states of others. This heightened empathy allows them to support better and understand the needs of their team members.

Social Skills: Reduced stress levels lead to improved communication and conflict resolution abilities. Project managers can maintain open and constructive dialogue with stakeholders and team members, leading to stronger relationships and better collaboration.

Stress management techniques are invaluable resources in the emotionally intelligent project manager's toolkit. By learning to navigate stress effectively, project managers can develop high emotional intelligence, enabling them to lead with clarity, empathy, and resilience. As they empower themselves through stress management, they also empower their projects and teams, driving success despite adversity. Ultimately, embracing stress management as an integral part of emotional intelligence equips project managers to tackle challenges head-on and achieve exceptional project outcomes.

Engaging Creative Outlets

Creativity and emotional intelligence are deeply intertwined. Engaging in creative pursuits allows project managers to tap into their emotional reservoirs, explore their feelings, and channel them into productive and positive outcomes. Creating art through painting, writing, or playing music fosters self-awareness and mindfulness – two fundamental components of emotional intelligence. When individuals become more in tune with their emotions, they can better recognize their strengths, limitations, triggers, and reactions.

Creative outlets also provide a safe space for project managers to express their emotions without judgment or restraint. This emotional release reduces stress and anxiety, improving emotional regulation and resilience in handling project challenges and team dynamics.

Cultivating Self-Awareness Through Creative Expression

Self-awareness is the cornerstone of emotional intelligence. Project managers who engage in creative outlets better understand their emotional patterns, values, and beliefs. For instance, painting allows them to visually represent their emotions and thoughts, while writing enables introspection and self-reflection. In this way, creative expression serves as a mirror that reflects their inner world, allowing them to identify emotional blind spots and make conscious efforts to improve their emotional intelligence.

Empathy and Understanding Others

Effective project management heavily relies on empathizing and understanding team members' perspectives and emotions. By practicing creative expression, project managers become more attuned to the emotions of others as well. For example, through writing stories or poems, they develop characters with distinct emotions and motivations, which fosters a deeper appreciation for the complexity of human emotions.

Playing music in a group setting also enhances empathy, requiring attentive listening and synchronization with other musicians. This heightened sense of empathy translates directly into project management scenarios, where understanding and connecting with team members on an emotional level can resolve conflicts, strengthen collaboration, and build trust.

Enhancing Communication Skills

Artistic pursuits involve communication through visual representation, storytelling, or musical interpretation. Engaging in creative outlets can improve project managers' ability to communicate effectively and persuasively. Writing helps refine written communication, while playing music sharpens non-verbal communication, such as body language and tone. These skills are invaluable in conveying project objectives, expectations, and feedback to stakeholders, clients, and team members.

Moreover, creative expression offers alternative avenues for communication, especially for project managers who might find it challenging to articulate their emotions verbally. The use of art can serve as a bridge for initiating difficult conversations or expressing gratitude, thereby fostering a more inclusive and emotionally intelligent project environment.

Stress Reduction and Burnout Prevention

The project management landscape can be intense, with tight deadlines, high-pressure situations, and demanding stakeholders. Engaging in creative outlets provides a healthy outlet for stress, reducing the risk of burnout. Painting, writing, and playing music are all meditative activities that encourage mindfulness and relaxation.

By integrating regular creative practices into their routines, project managers can build emotional resilience, better cope with stress, and maintain a clear and focused mindset amidst challenging situations.

Fostering Innovation and Problem-Solving Skills

Creativity and emotional intelligence complement each other in problem-solving and innovation. Creative outlets encourage divergent thinking, enabling project managers to approach challenges from different angles and find the best solutions. Writing, for instance, allows the exploration of multiple scenarios and potential outcomes, stimulating creativity in finding the best course of action.

Additionally, artistic pursuits often involve experimentation and embracing imperfections, teaching project managers to adopt a growth mindset when facing setbacks or unexpected roadblocks in their projects.

The power of creative outlets in building emotional intelligence for project managers cannot be understated. Painting, writing, and playing music are not merely hobbies or pastimes but essential tools for self-discovery, empathy, and communication. By engaging in these artistic endeavors, project managers gain a deeper understanding of their emotions, become more empathetic and understanding of others, enhance their communication skills, reduce stress and burnout, and foster innovation and problem-solving abilities.

As emotionally intelligent project managers embrace creativity and hone their emotional intelligence, they transform their approach to project management. By empowering themselves and their teams with emotional intelligence, they pave the way for successful projects that are not only delivered on time and within budget but also enriched with meaningful collaboration, trust, and satisfaction for all stakeholders involved.

Positive Affirmations

Positive affirmations are short, uplifting statements that reflect an individual's positive qualities, strengths, and aspirations. When consistently practiced, positive affirmations can transform a project manager's mindset and emotional well-being. The key lies in the power of self-talk – the internal dialogue that shapes how we perceive ourselves and the world around us.

Building Self-Awareness

Self-awareness is the foundation of emotional intelligence. Project managers in tune with their emotions and reactions can better understand how they influence their decision-making and behavior. Positive affirmations can foster self-awareness by encouraging project managers to reflect on their strengths and areas for growth. For instance, a project manager can repeat affirmations like "I am a confident and competent leader" or "I welcome challenges as chances for personal development and growth" By reinforcing these affirmations, project managers can gradually internalize these beliefs, leading to increased self-confidence and self-awareness.

Cultivating Self-Regulation

In the fast-paced world of project management, emotional triggers and stressful situations are inevitable. However, a project manager with solid self regulation skills can effectively manage their emotions and respond appropriately to challenging circumstances. Positive affirmations are a powerful tool in promoting self-regulation by creating a mental buffer against negativity. Repeating affirmations such as "I remain calm and composed under pressure" or "I respond with patience and understanding" helps project managers to reinforce positive behavior patterns, even during challenging times.

Enhancing Empathy

Empathy is essential for project managers to fully understand the needs and perspectives of their team members and stakeholders. Positive affirmations can aid in developing empathy by encouraging project managers to consider the feelings and experiences of others. Affirmations like "I actively listen and understand my team's concerns" or "I lead with compassion and respect" can remind project managers to prioritize empathy in their interactions, ultimately fostering stronger team relationships.

Strengthening Social Skills

Effective communication and interpersonal relationships are central to successful project management. Positive affirmations can bolster social skills by promoting positive communication patterns. Project managers can repeat affirmations such as "I communicate clearly and effectively" or "I inspire and motivate my team through my words and actions." These affirmations help project managers to build rapport and trust, encouraging open and constructive dialogue among team members.

Boosting Motivation

Project management can be challenging, and project managers often encounter obstacles that can dampen their enthusiasm. Positive affirmations are a powerful instrument for increasing motivation and maintaining a positive outlook. Affirmations like "I am resilient and persistent in achieving project goals" or "I stay focused and motivated, no matter the circumstances" can help project managers stay on track and maintain their enthusiasm, even in the face of adversity.

Emotional intelligence is not a static trait but a skill that can be cultivated and enhanced over time. Positive affirmations offer project managers a simple yet effective technique to increase their emotional intelligence and empower their projects. By integrating affirmations into their daily routine, project managers can develop self-awareness, self-regulation, empathy, social skills, and motivation. The regular practice of positive affirmations can lead to a profound transformation in how project managers perceive themselves and their interactions with others.

As project managers embrace positive affirmations, they embark on a journey of self-discovery and personal growth, ultimately leading to more emotionally intelligent and empowered project leaders. By harnessing the power of positive affirmations, project managers can create a work environment that nurtures emotional intelligence, fosters collaboration, and drives project success.

Identifying Emotional Triggers

Emotional triggers are catalysts for emotional responses. They can be positive and negative, from feeling inspired and motivated by a project's success to experiencing stress and frustration due to setbacks. Identifying emotional triggers involves developing self-awareness, which is the foundation of emotional intelligence. By being aware of their emotional triggers, project managers can gain valuable insights into their emotional patterns and reactions.

Self-Reflection for Enhanced Self-Awareness

Recognizing emotional triggers begins with self-reflection. Project managers must engage in regular introspection and ask themselves probing questions:

- What situations tend to evoke strong emotional responses in me?

- How do I react when things don't go as planned?

- Do certain team members or stakeholders trigger specific emotional reactions?

- What coping mechanisms do I use when faced with stress or pressure?

Project managers can record their emotions and responses during different project scenarios by keeping a journal or diary. This practice allows them to detect patterns and understand the underlying causes of their emotional triggers.

Acknowledging and Validating Emotions

Once emotional triggers are identified, project managers need to acknowledge and validate their emotions. Emotions are a natural and essential part of being human, and disregarding or suppressing them can be counterproductive. Emotions provide valuable information about a project manager's state of mind and can offer insights into their needs and expectations.

By acknowledging and validating emotions, project managers can foster a culture of open communication within their teams. Team members will feel more comfortable expressing their emotions, leading to a deeper understanding of each other's perspectives and concerns.

Practicing Emotional Regulation

While acknowledging emotions is crucial, emotional intelligence also involves effectively managing and regulating these emotions. Emotional regulation enables project managers to respond to challenging situations composed and constructively. This skill is precious during high-pressure moments when clear-headed decision-making is essential.

Various techniques can aid in emotional regulation:

a. Mindfulness: Encouraging project managers to be present in the moment and observe their emotions without judgment can prevent impulsive reactions.

b. Breathing exercises: Deep, intentional breathing can help project managers calm their nervous system and regain emotional balance.

c. Time-outs: Taking short breaks during tense situations can give project managers the necessary space to reflect on their emotions before responding.

Empathy and Understanding Others' Triggers

Emotional intelligence is not solely about understanding oneself but also empathizing with others. Project managers must try to identify emotional triggers in their team members and stakeholders. This empathetic approach allows project managers to be more supportive and understanding when dealing with emotionally charged situations.

Active listening and open communication are crucial in understanding others' emotional triggers. When team members feel heard and validated, it fosters trust and collaboration, which are essential for project success.

Identifying emotional triggers is fundamental to increasing emotional intelligence for project managers. Self-awareness, acknowledgment of emotions, emotional regulation, and empathy form the cornerstones of this process. By recognizing their emotional triggers, project managers can create a positive work environment fostering open communication, empathy, and resilience.

Empowered with emotional intelligence, project managers can navigate complex human interactions, build strong and cohesive teams, and steer their projects toward success. In the ever-evolving landscape of project management, emotional intelligence emerges as a vital skill distinguishing extraordinary project managers from the rest. Embracing emotional intelligence enables project managers to lead with compassion, understanding, and wisdom, propelling their projects to new heights of achievement and fulfillment.

Communications

Communication is a key role for an emotionally intelligent project manager. A project manager who possesses superior communication skills can navigate through challenges with finesse and inspire their team to reach new heights of collaboration and productivity. The good news is that these communication skills are not innate but can be acquired and honed through dedicated learning and practice. By cultivating these skills, project managers can create an environment of trust and understanding, paving the way for seamless project execution and fostering long-term success for their teams and organizations alike. The following are some vital skills that can help you grow your emotional intelligence.

Active Listening

Active listening is a communication technique that requires giving full attention to the speaker, processing the information received, and providing appropriate feedback. Unlike passive listening, where one merely hears the words spoken, active listening requires genuine engagement and involvement in the conversation. Project managers who actively listen show respect for their team members' perspectives, encourage open communication, and promote a culture of trust and empathy within the project team.

Building Trust and Empathy

In any project setting, trust is paramount. When project managers practice active listening, they make team members feel valued and heard. By carefully attending to what team members say, project managers create an atmosphere of respect and empathy, which fosters trust among team members. This trust becomes the foundation for open and honest communication, allowing project managers to understand their team's emotional state better.

Moreover, active listening helps project managers develop empathy—a vital part of emotional intelligence. Empathy is understanding and looking at things from the other person's viewpoint. It enables project managers to put themselves in their team members' shoes, grasping their concerns and joys. By demonstrating empathy, project managers create a positive work environment that encourages team members to be more engaged and committed to the project's success.

Enhancing Communication

Effective communication is vital for project managers to articulate their vision, goals, and expectations clearly. However, communication is not just about conveying messages—it is also about comprehending the messages received from others. Active listening enables project managers to listen attentively to team members' ideas, feedback, and concerns. By doing so, project managers can avoid misunderstandings, resolve conflicts proactively, and adapt their leadership style to meet individual team members' needs.

Additionally, active listening helps project managers identify non-verbal cues, such as body language and tone of voice, which often convey emotions more powerfully than words alone. Understanding these non-verbal cues is critical for project managers to gauge the emotional state of their team members and address any underlying issues that may hinder project progress.

Improving Problem-Solving and Decision-Making

Every project faces challenges, and a successful project manager's ability to handle these obstacles effectively is a defining characteristic. Active listening equips project managers with the necessary information to make the best decisions and solve problems efficiently. By actively listening to team members' ideas and concerns, project managers gain diverse perspectives that can lead to innovative solutions.

Moreover, active listening helps project managers identify potential risks and roadblocks early on, reducing the chances of project delays or failures. When team members feel comfortable sharing their thoughts, concerns, and suggestions, they contribute to a collaborative problem-solving approach, leading to more successful outcomes.

Strengthening Team Collaboration

Project managers who actively listen create a positive team dynamic where every team member feels valued and empowered. This inclusive approach strengthens team collaboration and enhances group cohesion. Active listening encourages open discussions and brainstorming sessions, fostering a culture where team members feel comfortable contributing their ideas without fear of judgment.

Furthermore, when team members see their project manager actively engaging in discussions and incorporating their feedback, they are more likely to be motivated and committed to the project's objectives. This higher motivation can lead to an increase in productivity and a higher quality of work.

Handling Emotional Conflicts

In any project, conflicts are bound to arise. These conflicts may arise from differences in opinions, different ways people work, or personal issues. Active listening equips project managers with the skills to manage emotional conflicts constructively. By actively listening to team members during conflicts, project managers demonstrate respect and empathy, reducing the emotional intensity of the situation.

Additionally, active listening allows project managers to uncover the underlying causes of conflicts and address them at their roots. By understanding the emotions and concerns of each team member involved in the conflict, project managers can mediate disputes more effectively and find resolutions that satisfy all parties.

Active listening is a powerful tool that can significantly increase a project manager's emotional intelligence. By actively engaging with team members, project managers build trust, empathy, and understanding within their project teams. This heightened emotional intelligence empowers project managers to communicate effectively, solve problems efficiently, and foster a collaborative work environment.

As project managers embrace active listening and emotional intelligence, they create an atmosphere where team members feel valued, heard, and motivated to contribute their best efforts. Ultimately, the emotionally intelligent project manager becomes a catalyst for empowered projects that achieve outstanding results while nurturing a cohesive and resilient team.

Non-Judgmental Language

Non-judgmental language involves communicating without imposing personal biases, assumptions, or preconceptions about others. It is a communication style that fosters openness, empathy, and understanding. When project managers use non-judgmental language, they refrain from criticizing, blaming, or making assumptions about team members' intentions or capabilities. Instead, they focus on active listening and seek to understand others' points of view and the emotions that come with them nonjudgmentally.

Cultivating Empathy and Understanding

Project managers who employ non-judgmental language create an environment where team members feel safe communicating their ideas and concerns. By avoiding judgmental remarks, project managers show that they respect individual differences and value diverse viewpoints. This fosters a culture of empathy and understanding within the team, enabling better collaboration and conflict resolution.

When team members feel their voices are heard, they are more likely to share their ideas, identify potential challenges, and work together to find innovative solutions. A non-judgmental approach encourages open dialogue, improving team dynamics and enhancing project performance.

Promoting Psychological Safety

Psychological safety is a critical factor in high-performing teams. When individuals experience a sense of psychological safety, they are more open to taking risks, experimenting with new approaches, and sharing their vulnerabilities. Non-judgmental language plays a pivotal role in creating a psychologically safe environment.

Project managers who refrain from passing judgment create a safe space where team members can openly express their concerns, admit mistakes, and seek support when needed. This openness increases trust among team members and the project manager, fostering a collaborative and supportive atmosphere where everyone feels valued and respected.

Conflict Resolution and Problem-Solving

In any project, conflicts are inevitable. However, how disputes are addressed can significantly affect project outcomes. Non-judgmental language allows project managers to approach conflicts with a level-headed and understanding demeanor.

By avoiding judgment and blame, project managers can focus on the underlying issues causing the conflict and work toward finding constructive solutions. Non-judgmental communication encourages team members to engage in productive discussions, leading to resolving disputes that benefit the entire team.

Building Trust and Credibility

Trust is the cornerstone of effective leadership. When project managers use non-judgmental language consistently, they build trust and credibility with their team. Trust is earned by showing genuine interest in team members' well-being and demonstrating that their concerns and opinions are valued.

When team members trust their project manager, they are more likely to be committed to the project's success and demonstrate higher motivation and engagement. Trust also encourages open communication, allowing project managers to receive valuable feedback and insights from the team.

Fostering Inclusive Communication

Inclusive communication is essential for projects that involve diverse teams with members from different cultural backgrounds, experiences, and perspectives. Non-judgmental language fosters inclusivity by respecting individual differences and promoting an environment where everyone feels welcome and accepted.

Project managers who embrace non-judgmental language actively seek input from all team members, valuing the richness of diverse ideas. This creates a sense of belonging and empowerment, enhancing team cohesion and leading to more innovative and successful project outcomes.

A non-judgmental language is a powerful tool for project managers seeking to enhance their emotional intelligence and empower their projects. Project managers can create a positive and high-performing team culture by cultivating empathy, promoting psychological safety, resolving conflicts effectively, building trust, and fostering inclusive communication.

As project managers become more attuned to their communication styles and strive to use non-judgmental language consistently, they will experience a profound impact on team dynamics, collaboration, and overall project success. Embracing non-judgmental language is not only a sign of emotional intelligence but also a testament to a project manager's commitment to creating a work environment that celebrates diversity encourages open communication, and values the contributions of each team member. Project managers can empower projects through emotional intelligence by integrating non-judgmental language into their leadership approach.

Appreciative Communications

Appreciative communication is a style of interaction that focuses on recognizing and valuing team members' contributions, efforts, and achievements. Instead of dwelling on problems or shortcomings, the emotionally intelligent project manager seeks to uplift and celebrate successes. By implementing appreciative communications, project managers can create a positive and supportive atmosphere that boosts team morale and fosters a sense of camaraderie.

Shifting Focus to Positivity

Project managers can start by shifting the team's focus from identifying problems to acknowledging successes and positive outcomes. This change in approach can be implemented during team meetings, performance evaluations, or even casual interactions with team members. The project manager reinforces a culture of appreciation by highlighting accomplishments and expressing gratitude for everyone's hard work.

Encouraging Open Appreciation

An emotionally intelligent project manager openly expresses appreciation and encourages team members to do the same. This can be achieved through regular expressions of gratitude, personalized notes of acknowledgment, or public recognition during team gatherings. When team members feel valued and recognized for their efforts, they become more engaged and committed to the project's success.

Active Listening and Empathy

Appreciative communication involves active listening and empathetic understanding. When team members feel someone is truly listening to them and understanding what they are saying, they are more likely to share their thoughts and ideas freely. An emotionally intelligent project manager demonstrates genuine interest in the concerns and opinions of others, creating an environment of trust and a safe place to have discussions.

Constructive Feedback with Positive Reinforcement

Feedback is essential to project management, but an emotionally intelligent project manager balances constructive criticism with positive reinforcement. Instead of pointing out errors, the project manager identifies improvement areas while acknowledging the individual's strengths and past achievements. This approach encourages a growth mindset and motivates team members to perform better.

Benefits of Appreciative Communications and Positive Reinforcement

Implementing appreciative communication and positive reinforcement in project management yields numerous benefits for the project manager and the entire team.

Increased Team Morale and Motivation

A positive and supportive work environment, created through appreciative communications, boosts team morale and motivation.

When team members sense recognition and worth, their enthusiasm for their work increases, and they become more dedicated to ensuring the success of the project.

Strengthened Team Collaboration

Appreciative communication fosters more vital team collaboration and cohesion. Team members feel a connection with each other and work collaboratively towards a common purpose, creating a sense of unity and trust within the team.

Higher Productivity and Performance

When team members feel appreciated and motivated, their productivity and performance improve. Positive reinforcement is a powerful incentive, encouraging individuals to put forth their best efforts and strive for excellence.

Reduced Conflict and Stress

Emotionally intelligent project managers who practice appreciative communication are more adept at resolving conflicts and reducing stress within the team. By acknowledging the efforts of team members and addressing concerns empathetically, they create a harmonious and supportive work environment.

Enhanced Stakeholder Relations

Positive reinforcement and appreciation extend beyond the team to project stakeholders. Recognizing stakeholders' contributions and showing gratitude for their support can strengthen relationships and lead to tremendous project success.

Appreciative communication and positive reinforcement are essential tools that can significantly enhance a project manager's emotional intelligence and, consequently, the overall project's success. By focusing on positivity, expressing genuine appreciation, and balancing feedback with acknowledgment of strengths, the emotionally intelligent project manager empowers the team, fosters a collaborative work environment, and achieves superior results. In an ever-changing and challenging project landscape, emotional intelligence remains a key differentiator that sets successful project managers apart.

Tone of Voice

Appreciative communication is a style of interaction that focuses on recognizing and valuing team members' contributions, efforts, and achievements. Instead of dwelling on problems or shortcomings, the emotionally intelligent project manager seeks to uplift and celebrate successes. By implementing appreciative communications, project managers can create a positive and supportive atmosphere that boosts team morale and fosters a sense of camaraderie.

Shifting Focus to Positivity

Project managers can start by shifting the team's focus from identifying problems to acknowledging successes and positive outcomes. This change in approach can be implemented during team meetings, performance evaluations, or even casual interactions with team members. The project manager reinforces a culture of appreciation by highlighting accomplishments and expressing gratitude for everyone's hard work.

Encouraging Open Appreciation

An emotionally intelligent project manager openly expresses appreciation and encourages team members to do the same. This can be achieved through regular expressions of gratitude, personalized notes of acknowledgment, or public recognition during team gatherings. When team members feel valued and recognized for their efforts, they become more engaged and committed to the project's success.

Active Listening and Empathy

Appreciative communication involves active listening and empathetic understanding. When team members feel someone is truly listening to them and understanding what they are saying, they are more likely to share their thoughts and ideas freely. An emotionally intelligent project manager demonstrates genuine interest in the concerns and opinions of others, creating an environment of trust and a safe place to have discussions.

Constructive Feedback with Positive Reinforcement

Feedback is essential to project management, but an emotionally intelligent project manager balances constructive criticism with positive reinforcement. Instead of pointing out errors, the project manager identifies improvement areas while acknowledging the individual's strengths and past achievements. This approach encourages a growth mindset and motivates team members to perform better.

Benefits of Appreciative Communications and Positive Reinforcement

Implementing appreciative communication and positive reinforcement in project management yields numerous benefits for the project manager and the entire team.

Increased Team Morale and Motivation

A positive and supportive work environment, created through appreciative communications, boosts team morale and motivation. When team members sense recognition and worth, their enthusiasm for their work increases, and they become more dedicated to ensuring the success of the project.

Strengthened Team Collaboration

Appreciative communication fosters more vital team collaboration and cohesion. Team members feel a connection with each other and work collaboratively towards a common purpose, creating a sense of unity and trust within the team.

Higher Productivity and Performance

When team members feel appreciated and motivated, their productivity and performance improve. Positive reinforcement is a powerful incentive, encouraging individuals to put forth their best efforts and strive for excellence.

Reduced Conflict and Stress

Emotionally intelligent project managers who practice appreciative communication are more adept at resolving conflicts and reducing stress within the team. By acknowledging the efforts of team members and addressing concerns empathetically, they create a harmonious and supportive work environment.

Enhanced Stakeholder Relations

Positive reinforcement and appreciation extend beyond the team to project stakeholders. Recognizing stakeholders' contributions and showing gratitude for their support can strengthen relationships and lead to tremendous project success.

Appreciative communication and positive reinforcement are essential tools that can significantly enhance a project manager's emotional intelligence and, consequently, the overall project's success. By focusing on positivity, expressing genuine appreciation, and balancing feedback with acknowledgment of strengths, the emotionally intelligent project manager empowers the team, fosters a collaborative work environment, and achieves superior results. In an ever-changing and challenging project landscape, emotional intelligence remains a key differentiator that sets successful project managers apart.

Openness to Feedbackeedback is a vital tool in developing emotional intelligence, as it acts as a mirror, reflecting strengths and areas that need improvement. When a project manager receives feedback, it allows them to assess their behavior and performance from an outside perspective. By embracing feedback with an open mind, project managers can recognize blind spots, understand how their actions impact others, and adapt their approach accordingly.

Cultivating Self-Awareness

Self-awareness is the first pillar of emotional intelligence, and feedback is a critical driver in its cultivation. When team members and stakeholders provide constructive feedback, project managers gain insights into the style of leadership, how they communicate, and their decision-making processes. This awareness enables them to recognize their emotions as they arise and understand how they influence their behavior. With increased self-awareness, project managers can prevent impulsive reactions and make more thoughtful decisions, leading to more successful project outcomes.

Strengthening Emotional Resilience

In high-pressure project management, emotional resilience is essential for overcoming challenges and setbacks. Whether positive or negative, feedback can be an emotional trigger for project managers. Project managers can build their emotional resilience over time by actively seeking feedback and staying open to it. They learn to handle criticism constructively and use it as a stepping stone for improvement rather than allowing it to impact their self-esteem or motivation negatively.

Empathy and Understanding

Embracing feedback benefits project managers and reinforces a culture of open communication and trust within the team. When team members observe their project manager being receptive to feedback, it fosters a sense of psychological safety, encouraging them to share their thoughts and concerns openly. This exchange of feedback promotes empathy and understanding between the project manager and team members, leading to better collaboration, reduced conflicts, and increased overall team performance.

Continuous Learning and Growth

Project management is an ever-evolving field, and a successful project manager must be committed to continuous learning and growth. Embracing feedback serves as a powerful catalyst for ongoing development. Actively seeking feedback from team members, superiors, and even external stakeholders allows project managers to identify areas of improvement and build upon their strengths. This commitment to growth enhances their emotional intelligence and helps them stay ahead of industry trends and best practices, benefiting the project and the organization.

Emotional intelligence is critical for project managers seeking to empower their projects and teams to achieve greatness. Being open to feedback is a fundamental aspect of developing emotional intelligence, as it enables project managers to cultivate self-awareness, strengthen emotional resilience, foster empathy, and embrace continuous learning. By actively seeking and valuing feedback, project managers can create an environment of trust, collaboration, and growth, resulting in more successful and satisfying project outcomes.

Emotional intelligence will remain a cornerstone of effective leadership as the project management landscape evolves. Project managers who recognize the transformative power of feedback and integrate it into their professional journey will undoubtedly thrive in an ever-changing and demanding industry, leaving a lasting impact on their projects and the individuals they lead.

Paraphrasing

Feedback is a vital tool in developing emotional intelligence, as it acts as a mirror, reflecting strengths and areas that need improvement. When a project manager receives feedback, it allows them to assess their behavior and performance from an outside perspective. By embracing feedback with an open mind, project managers can recognize blind spots, understand how their actions impact others, and adapt their approach accordingly.

Cultivating Self-Awareness

Self-awareness is the first pillar of emotional intelligence, and feedback is a critical driver in its cultivation. When team members and stakeholders provide constructive feedback, project managers gain insights into the style of leadership, how they communicate, and their decision-making processes. This awareness enables them to recognize their emotions as they arise and understand how they influence their behavior. With increased self-awareness, project managers can prevent impulsive reactions and make more thoughtful decisions, leading to more successful project outcomes.

Strengthening Emotional Resilience

In high-pressure project management, emotional resilience is essential for overcoming challenges and setbacks. Whether positive or negative, feedback can be an emotional trigger for project managers. Project managers can build their emotional resilience over time by actively seeking feedback and staying open to it. They learn to handle criticism constructively and use it as a stepping stone for improvement rather than allowing it to impact their self-esteem or motivation negatively.

Empathy and Understanding

Embracing feedback benefits project managers and reinforces a culture of open communication and trust within the team. When team members observe their project manager being receptive to feedback, it fosters a sense of psychological safety, encouraging them to share their thoughts and concerns openly. This exchange of feedback promotes empathy and understanding between the project manager and team members, leading to better collaboration, reduced conflicts, and increased overall team performance.

Continuous Learning and Growth

Project management is an ever-evolving field, and a successful project manager must be committed to continuous learning and growth. Embracing feedback serves as a powerful catalyst for ongoing development. Actively seeking feedback from team members, superiors, and even external stakeholders allows project managers to identify areas of improvement and build upon their strengths. This commitment to growth enhances their emotional intelligence and helps them stay ahead of industry trends and best practices, benefiting the project and the organization.

Emotional intelligence is critical for project managers seeking to empower their projects and teams to achieve greatness. Being open to feedback is a fundamental aspect of developing emotional intelligence, as it enables project managers to cultivate self-awareness, strengthen emotional resilience, foster empathy, and embrace continuous learning. By actively seeking and valuing feedback, project managers can create an environment of trust, collaboration, and growth, resulting in more successful and satisfying project outcomes.

Emotional intelligence will remain a cornerstone of effective leadership as the project management landscape evolves. Project managers who recognize the transformative power of feedback and integrate it into their professional journey will undoubtedly thrive in an ever-changing and demanding industry, leaving a lasting impact on their projects and the individuals they lead.

Non-Verbal Cues & Emotional Intelligence

At the heart of emotional intelligence lies the art of communication, and while words are powerful, they constitute only a fraction of the exchange between individuals. Non-verbal cues, a universal language of emotions, form a substantial part of how we understand and connect. How we express ourselves through facial expressions, body language, and gestures often reveal more about our emotions than words alone can convey. In this section, we delve into the importance of non-verbal cues in emotional intelligence and explore how project managers can harness this unspoken language to empower projects and cultivate strong, cohesive teams.

Understanding the Essence of Non-Verbal Cues:

Non-verbal cues are like hidden gems that enrich our interactions, providing valuable insights into the emotions and intentions of others. Being attuned to these cues for project managers seeking to lead diverse teams becomes an indispensable skill. Recognizing the subtleties of non-verbal communication allows managers to comprehend better the unexpressed concerns, fears, and aspirations that may influence team members' performance and engagement.

The Influence of Non-Verbal Cues on Team Dynamics:

In any project, the dynamics among team members play a pivotal role in determining success. Emotions, if left unattended, can quickly escalate and jeopardize collaboration. However, by acknowledging and interpreting non-verbal cues, project managers can preempt and address potential conflicts before they escalate. The ability to read the room and empathize with team members' feelings lays the foundation for a more harmonious and productive work environment.

Non-Verbal Cues in Stakeholder Management:

Beyond the project team, successful project management also hinges on effective stakeholder engagement. Understanding the non-verbal cues exhibited by stakeholders during meetings and negotiations can provide invaluable insights into their reactions, expectations, and concerns. A project manager adept at decoding these cues can tailor their communication and decision-making strategies accordingly, thus enhancing the likelihood of stakeholder buy-in and support.

Leveraging Non-Verbal Cues for Inspirational Leadership:

Leadership is not solely about providing direction and guidance but inspiring and motivating others to achieve their best. An emotionally intelligent project manager utilizes non-verbal cues to connect on a deeper level with their team, showing genuine interest and understanding. Demonstrating empathy through non-verbal means creates an atmosphere of trust, empowerment, and mutual respect, fostering a sense of belonging that propels the team toward shared goals.

The Art of Non-Verbal Expression in Difficult Conversations:

Project managers inevitably face challenging situations that demand sensitive handling. Non-verbal cues become especially crucial in such moments, as they can ease or exacerbate tensions. Being mindful of one's non-verbal cues during difficult conversations and recognizing those of others allows project managers to maintain composure, exhibit emotional control, and convey a sense of empathy even in challenging circumstances.

As we explore non-verbal cues in emotional intelligence, it becomes clear that this unspoken language plays a central role in empowering projects and fostering cohesive, high-performing teams. By embracing the nuances of non-verbal communication, project managers can cultivate a work environment that nurtures emotional well-being, promotes understanding, and unlocks the full potential of their projects. Through this chapter, we aim to equip project managers with the tools to harness the power of non-verbal cues, elevating them to become genuinely emotionally intelligent leaders capable of driving meaningful, transformative change.

Eye Contact

Eye contact is one of the most powerful non-verbal cues in human communication. It is a subtle yet profound way to convey emotions, establish connections, and display attentiveness. When project managers master the art of meaningful eye contact, they can create an environment of trust and openness within their project teams. Here's how eye contact contributes to enhanced communication:

✓ Establishing Trust and Credibility: Maintaining eye contact during conversations conveys sincerity and honesty. Team members are more likely to trust a project manager who actively listens and engages through eye contact, fostering a sense of credibility and reliability.

✓ Demonstrating Active Listening: Meaningful eye contact signals the speaker that the project manager is fully present and actively listening. This encourages team members to express their ideas, concerns, and feedback openly, knowing their words are valued.

✓ Enhancing Understanding of Non-Verbal Cues: Much of the communication is non-verbal in face-to-face interactions. A project manager can better comprehend the emotions and unspoken messages behind team members' words by paying attention to eye movements and expressions.

✓ Encouraging Emotional Expression: Projects can be intense, and team members may experience various emotions throughout the journey. When a project manager maintains eye contact and shows empathy, team members are more likely to feel comfortable expressing their feelings, leading to better emotional support and problem-solving.

Empathy and Emotional Connection

Empathy, a core aspect of emotional intelligence, allows project managers to understand and see things from the perspective of team members. Meaningful eye contact is a crucial tool for expressing empathy and building emotional connections within the project team:

- Building Emotional Bridges: Meeting someone's gaze fosters a deeper emotional connection, making team members feel heard and understood. It bridges the gap between individuals, reducing misunderstandings and conflicts.

- Sensing Emotional States: Eye contact enables project managers to discern emotional cues more effectively. Deciphering these cues allows project managers to respond with appropriate support and encouragement during challenging times.

- Demonstrating Emotional Support: In times of stress or pressure, a simple gaze of reassurance can provide immense comfort to team members. It indicates that the project manager acknowledges their emotions and is there to support them.

Conflict Resolution and Diffusing Tension

Conflicts are an inevitable part of any project. How a project manager handles conflicts can significantly impact the team's dynamics and project outcomes. Eye contact can play a critical role in conflict resolution:

- Encouraging Constructive Dialogue: When resolving conflicts, maintaining eye contact with involved parties encourages them to engage in more respectful and constructive dialogue. It discourages hostile behavior and fosters a sense of mutual understanding.

- Minimizing Misinterpretations: Lack of eye contact might be misconstrued as disinterest or indifference during conflict discussions. On the other hand, maintaining eye contact portrays active engagement and a willingness to find a resolution.

- Demonstrating Emotional Maturity: A project manager who can hold eye contact while addressing conflicts displays emotional maturity. This behavior encourages team members to follow suit, leading to a more emotionally intelligent team dynamic.

The power of eye contact cannot be understated in the journey of an emotionally intelligent project manager. As a critical element of non-verbal communication, eye contact enables project managers to establish trust, enhance understanding, and build meaningful connections with their team members. By harnessing this essential skill, project managers can elevate their emotional intelligence and empower their projects to thrive. Remember, eye contact is about seeing with the eyes and understanding with the heart. The emotionally intelligent project manager recognizes this and uses it as a guiding principle to lead their team to success.

Facial Expressions

Facial expressions are the focal of nonverbal communication that conveys emotions and feelings. People instinctively respond to facial cues, making them essential for understanding others' emotional states and intentions. As a project manager, reading and interpreting facial expressions enables you to connect with team members deeper, leading to better collaboration and team cohesion.

The Role of Facial Expressions in Emotional Intelligence

a. Self-Awareness: Recognizing your emotions is the first step towards emotional intelligence. Paying close attention to your facial expressions can provide critical insights into your emotional state. Awareness of how your emotions manifest on your face empowers you to regulate them better, especially in high-stress situations.

b. Self-Management: Controlling one's emotions is crucial for effective project management. Understanding the impact of your facial expressions on others enables you to adjust your responses appropriately. For instance, maintaining a calm and composed facial demeanor during times of crisis can instill confidence in your team, fostering a sense of security and stability.

c. Social Awareness: Being attuned to the facial expressions of team members and stakeholders allows you to gauge their emotional states accurately. Empathizing with their feelings and concerns builds trust and promotes open communication, which is vital for proactively addressing potential issues.

d. Relationship Management: Positive relationships are the backbone of successful projects. Project managers who can interpret the facial expressions of team members can detect signs of dissatisfaction, frustration, or enthusiasm. Project managers can strengthen team relationships and foster a sense of belonging by addressing these emotions and promoting a supportive atmosphere.

Recognizing Different Facial Expressions

A project manager's ability to recognize and interpret different facial expressions is fundamental to enhancing emotional intelligence. Common facial expressions conveying emotions include:

a. Happiness: A genuine smile, with the corners of the mouth and eyes raised, signifies happiness and contentment.

b. Sadness: A downturned mouth, drooping eyelids, and a furrowed brow indicate sadness or disappointment.

c. Anger: A tense jaw, narrowed eyes, and a furrowed forehead indicate anger or frustration.

d. Surprise: Widened eyes and an open mouth convey surprise or astonishment.

e. Fear: Raised eyebrows, widened eyes, and a stiff and rigid mouth indicate fear or anxiety.

f. Disgust: A curled lip and wrinkled nose suggest disgust or aversion.

Cultivating Emotional Intelligence Through Facial Expressions

Project managers can proactively develop their emotional intelligence by integrating facial expression awareness into their daily interactions:

a. Active Listening: Observe team members' facial expressions during team meetings or individual conversations. Active listening combined with facial expression interpretation can help you understand their perspectives, even when they are hesitant to voice their concerns.

b. Empathy and Compassion: Display empathy through your facial expressions when team members express their emotions. Show that you understand their feelings, reinforcing a supportive and understanding work environment.

c. Emotional Regulation: Practice regulating facial expressions, especially in stressful situations. Maintain a composed demeanor to avoid spreading panic or anxiety to the team.

d. Encourage Open Communication: Create a culture that encourages open expression of emotions and opinions. Please make yourself approachable so team members feel secure in sharing their thoughts and concerns.

e. Cross-Cultural Considerations: Be aware that facial expressions are not common across cultures. Some expressions may vary across cultures, so understanding these distinctions can prevent misinterpretation.

Facial expressions are a potent yet often overlooked tool for project managers seeking to increase their emotional intelligence. By becoming adept at reading and interpreting facial cues, project managers can develop a deeper understanding of themselves and their team members, fostering stronger relationships and more successful projects. Integrating facial expression awareness into everyday interactions empowers project managers to lead with empathy, authenticity, and resilience, driving their teams toward greater success and fulfillment. In the ever-evolving world of project management, embracing emotional intelligence through facial expressions is a valuable asset that can set exceptional project managers apart.

Smiling

The smile transcends cultures and is understood as a positive emotion, and its impact extends far beyond a simple gesture. It can convey warmth, acceptance, and encouragement, creating an atmosphere of trust and cooperation within the project team. As project managers constantly face challenges, deadlines, and conflicts, using a smile strategically becomes an invaluable asset.

Building Rapport and Trust

A smiling project manager is approachable and inviting. When team members feel comfortable coming to their manager with ideas, concerns, or problems, it fosters open communication and trust. This trust empowers team members to take responsibility for their tasks, improving collaboration and project performance.

Diffusing Tension and Conflicts

Conflicts are inevitable in any project, and how they are handled significantly impacts the project's outcome. A project manager who can smile in the face of conflict can ease tension and reduce emotional stress. Smiling communicates a willingness to listen and understand, promoting a more constructive approach to conflict resolution.

Enhancing Team Morale

The emotional state of a project manager has a direct influence on the team's morale. A smiling and cheerful project manager can boost team spirit, motivation, and engagement. Team members feel appreciated and valued, increasing job satisfaction and productivity.

Encouraging Creativity and Innovation

A smile creates a psychologically welcoming environment where team members feel comfortable expressing their ideas without fear or ridicule. This psychological safety encourages creativity and innovation, leading to novel solutions and improved project outcomes.

Modeling Emotional Regulation

Emotional intelligence involves recognizing and regulating one's emotions effectively. By smiling even during challenging situations, a project manager sets an example of emotional resilience for the team. This behavior reinforces the importance of emotional self-control and inspires team members to adopt similar practices.

Improving Client and Stakeholder Relations

Project managers often interact with various stakeholders and clients throughout a project's lifecycle. A genuine smile can leave a lasting positive impression on them. It signals attentiveness, professionalism, and a commitment to building solid relationships, which can lead to increased support, resources, and future collaboration.

Empathy and Understanding

A smiling project manager empathizes and understands team members' emotions and concerns. By acknowledging their feelings, the manager can address emotional needs appropriately, thus strengthening the bonds within the team.

In project management, emotional intelligence is a fundamental skill that empowers project managers to lead effectively and create a thriving work environment. A simple smile is a powerful and versatile tool among the many tools that enhance emotional intelligence.

Project managers can build rapport, trust, and positive relationships with their team members and stakeholders by understanding the significance of a smile and utilizing it strategically. Smiling helps diffuse tension, enhances team morale, and encourages an environment of creativity and innovation. Moreover, a smiling project manager sets an example of emotional regulation and empathy, fostering an environment of emotional intelligence throughout the project team.

Body Posture

Body posture, the way we hold ourselves and move, communicates information about our emotional state and influences how others perceive and respond to us. In this chapter, we will explore how body posture can significantly contribute to a project manager's emotional intelligence and, in turn, lead to more successful project outcomes.

Understanding the Link between Body Posture and Emotions

As social beings, humans communicate nonverbally through body language. Our posture not only reflects our emotions but also influences our emotional state. For example, a slouched posture may indicate feelings of defeat or disinterest, whereas an open and upright posture can convey confidence and assertiveness. Becoming aware of these cues can help project managers gain insights into their own emotions and those of others, fostering better communication and empathy.

The Impact of Body Posture on Project Team Dynamics

In a project environment, team dynamics are pivotal in achieving objectives. How project managers carry themselves can significantly impact team morale and motivation. Project managers who display positive and open body postures create an environment that encourages trust and approachability, making team members more likely to share ideas, concerns, and feedback.

Moreover, mirroring is a natural human tendency where individuals unconsciously mimic the body language of the person they are interacting with. By maintaining a composed and optimistic body posture, project managers can encourage their team members to adopt similar postures, promoting a positive emotional atmosphere and fostering a sense of unity within the team.

Using Body Posture to Manage Stress and Pressure

Project management can be high-stress, filled with tight deadlines and demanding stakeholders. A project manager's body posture can exacerbate or alleviate stress during challenging situations. Consciously adopting a relaxed and grounded posture, even during pressure moments, can help project managers remain calm and focused.

By recognizing the interplay between body posture and emotions, project managers can develop mindfulness practices that enable them to respond rather than react to stressors. Techniques such as deep breathing, maintaining an open chest, and avoiding tense postures can help project managers manage stress effectively and make better decisions under pressure.

Body Posture in Conflict Resolution

Conflicts are inevitable in project management, and how a project manager handles them can significantly impact team dynamics and project progress. When engaging in conflict resolution, displaying open body language and active listening signals a willingness to understand the concerns of all parties involved.

Moreover, adopting a non-threatening posture, such as avoiding crossed arms or invading personal space, can prevent conflicts from escalating and create a safe environment where team members feel comfortable expressing their emotions and concerns. A project manager who demonstrates empathy through body posture is likelier to find constructive resolutions to conflicts and strengthen team relationships.

Leveraging Body Posture in Stakeholder Management

Effective stakeholder management is a critical aspect of successful project execution. Project managers need to engage and influence stakeholders to gain support and resources. Body posture can significantly impact stakeholder perceptions and reactions during interactions.

Maintaining an open and confident posture enhances the project manager's credibility when presenting project updates or proposals. Strong eye contact and confident gestures convey conviction in the project's success. This, in turn, can evoke positive emotions in stakeholders and increase their confidence in the project manager's abilities.

Building Empathy through Body Posture

Empathy, the ability to understand and share the feelings of others, is a central component of emotional intelligence. Body posture can be a powerful tool for developing empathy. When engaging with team members, project managers should observe their body language to detect underlying emotions and respond appropriately.

Mirroring team members' body language during conversations can create a sense of rapport and connectedness, fostering an environment where team members feel understood and supported. By consciously using body posture to empathize with their team, project managers can build stronger relationships and create a more collaborative and emotionally intelligent work environment.

As project managers seek to enhance their emotional intelligence, they must recognize the profound impact that body posture can have on their effectiveness as leaders. Consciously employing positive and empathetic body language can strengthen team dynamics, improve stakeholder communication, and facilitate conflict resolution.

The power of body posture lies in its ability to enhance emotional intelligence through improved self-awareness and heightened interpersonal connections. By leveraging this often-overlooked aspect of communication, project managers can empower their projects and lead their teams to success with emotional intelligence as their guiding force.

Handshake

A handshake is a universal gesture of greeting, agreement, and connection. It is an age-old symbol of trust and mutual respect across cultures. The significance of the handshake goes beyond a mere formality; it creates an opportunity for project managers to connect on a deeper level with their team members and stakeholders. By mastering the art of the handshake, project managers can leverage this physical gesture to enhance their emotional intelligence and empower their projects.

Building Trust and Rapport

Emotional intelligence is at the heart of building trust and rapport with others. A handshake can be a powerful icebreaker that sets the tone for positive interactions. When a project manager extends a warm and firm handshake to team members and stakeholders, it creates a sense of trust and establishes a foundation for open communication. This physical connection signals the project manager is approachable, respectful, and genuinely interested in forging a solid working relationship.

Reading Non-Verbal Cues

An emotionally intelligent project manager possesses great empathy and is skilled at reading non-verbal cues. The act of shaking hands allows the project manager to gain valuable insights into the emotions of others. A limp handshake might indicate nervousness or lack of confidence, while a firm and enthusiastic handshake can reflect a positive attitude and eagerness to engage. By paying attention to these subtle cues, project managers can adjust their communication style and adapt to the emotional needs of their team members.

Fostering Team Cohesion

Projects often involve diverse teams with varying personalities and communication styles. A project manager with high emotional intelligence can bring together a cohesive team by acknowledging individual differences and promoting a sense of belonging. A simple handshake during team meetings or one-on-one interactions fosters a feeling of unity and inclusiveness. It reminds team members that they are all part of a shared vision and encourages collaboration.

Conflict Resolution and Negotiation

Conflict is inevitable in any project, and an emotionally intelligent project manager must be equipped to handle it effectively. The handshake can serve as a tool for conflict resolution and negotiation. During tense situations, initiating a handshake can help ease tensions and demonstrate the project manager's willingness to find common ground. It also reinforces the idea that despite differences, the project manager values and respects the opinions and contributions of all team members.

Empathy and Emotional Support

An emotionally intelligent project manager understands that team members are not just resources but individuals with emotions and concerns. When team members face personal or professional challenges, a handshake accompanied by a compassionate word or a supportive gesture can provide emotional support. This small act can build trust and loyalty, fostering a work environment where team members feel valued and cared for.

The handshake is a simple yet powerful tool for enhancing emotional intelligence for project managers. By understanding the symbolism and power behind this gesture, project managers can leverage it to build trust, foster team cohesion, read non-verbal cues, resolve conflicts, and provide emotional support to their team members. As project managers master the art of the handshake, they will be better equipped to navigate the complexities of interpersonal relationships and empower their projects through emotional intelligence. Remember, a single handshake can be the catalyst that transforms a project manager from competent to genuinely exceptional.

Emotional Intelligence and Working Remotely

In today's rapidly evolving world, project managers face the challenge of managing remote projects and teams more frequently than ever before. Technology advancements have transformed how teams collaborate, communicate, and execute tasks across geographical boundaries. With the rise of remote work and the growing emphasis on emotional intelligence in project management, integrating technology and emotional intelligence has become essential for empowering projects to succeed. This chapter delves into how project managers can leverage technology to enhance emotional intelligence and effectively manage remote projects and teams.

Understanding the Shift to Remote Work

The shift to remote work has redefined traditional project management practices. Project managers must realize that this is the new normal and adapt their strategies accordingly. By understanding the reasons behind remote work's popularity, project managers can better appreciate the significance of leveraging technology to facilitate effective management. Some reasons for the rise of remote work include increased employee satisfaction, access to a larger pool of qualified people, and money-saving opportunities for businesses.

Virtual Collaboration Platforms

The foundation of successful remote project management lies in establishing seamless communication channels. Virtual collaboration platforms serve as centralized hubs where team members can interact, share ideas, and collaborate on real-time project tasks. Tools like Slack, Microsoft Teams, or Asana allow project managers to create dedicated discussions, file-sharing, and task-tracking spaces.

Video Conferencing and Real-Time Communication

Face-to-face interaction fosters stronger connections among team members. Video conferencing tools like Zoom, Google Meet, or Microsoft Teams enable project managers to conduct virtual meetings that mimic in-person gatherings. The ability to see facial expressions and body language enhances communication and emotional understanding, reducing the chances of misunderstandings and misinterpretations.

Task and Project Management Software

Task and project management software are indispensable to keep remote projects on track. These tools help project managers assign tasks, set deadlines, and monitor progress efficiently. Platforms like Trello, Asana, Jira, or Basecamp provide transparency into project timelines and individual responsibilities, fostering a sense of accountability among team members.

Emotional Intelligence Assessments and Training

Project managers can leverage emotional intelligence and personality assessments to gauge team members' emotional intelligence levels and identify areas for improvement. Additionally, offering emotional intelligence training through webinars, online courses, or coaching sessions can empower team members to develop their emotional intelligence skills, improving team dynamics.

Data Analytics for Performance Insights

Technology also allows project managers to collect and analyze team performance and project outcomes data. By leveraging data analytics tools, project managers can gain valuable insights into team dynamics, identify potential bottlenecks, and make data-driven decisions to optimize project efficiency and collaboration.

Embracing technology in remote project management enables project managers to leverage emotional intelligence and empower their teams to succeed. By integrating virtual collaboration platforms, video conferencing tools, task and project management software, emotional intelligence assessments, and gamification techniques, project managers can foster effective communication, collaboration, and motivation within remote teams. Additionally, data analytics empowers project managers to gain valuable insights into team performance, leading to continuous improvement and enhanced project outcomes.

To become genuinely emotionally intelligent project managers, leaders must understand the importance of technology in remote project management and embrace its capabilities to nurture emotional intelligence within themselves and their teams. As technology advances, project managers who effectively integrate it with emotional intelligence will undoubtedly be better equipped to empower their projects and lead their teams to greater heights in the dynamic and ever-evolving professional landscape.

Conclusion

Thank you for reading **"Beyond the Gantt Chart: The Human Element of Project Management Success through Emotional Intelligence."** As we close out, I hope we showed – the immense impact of emotional intelligence on project success and the individuals involved.

Throughout this journey, we have explored the boundless potential that lies within every project manager, waiting to be unlocked through their hidden superpower of emotional intelligence. We discovered that technical skills alone do not guarantee success; the fusion of emotional intelligence and technical skills propels projects and project managers toward greatness.

Initially, we set the foundation by unraveling the essence of emotional intelligence—understanding its significance, the power it holds to transform projects, and the very nature of our leadership style. We explored how emotional intelligence empowers project managers to forge deeper connections, foster a harmonious team dynamic, and navigate complexities with finesse.

Throughout these chapters, we discovered the immense benefits of emotional intelligence in project management, enabling us to cultivate resilience, adaptability, and empathy as guiding principles in our professional lives. We recognized that embracing emotional intelligence is not a sign of vulnerability but a testament to our strength and wisdom as leaders.

As we explored the realm of self-awareness, we utilized the Color Code personality tool to gain deeper insights into our emotional tendencies, helping us understand ourselves and others with greater clarity. This self-awareness equipped us with the tools to overcome challenges and inspire positive change.

Our journey didn't stop there. We delved into the management tools that emotional intelligence bestows upon us, equipping project managers with powerful skills to foster collaboration, manage conflicts, and promote a thriving project environment.

Moreover, we recognized the indispensable role of effective communication in the emotional intelligence repertoire. By mastering the art of emotional intelligence in our conversations, we create bridges of understanding and trust, elevating our leadership to new heights.

Not even non-verbal cues escaped our attention as we learned to decipher the unspoken language of emotions, enabling us to attune ourselves to the needs and feelings of those around us.

Finally, in a rapidly evolving world, we embraced the relevance of emotional intelligence in the remote environment. We discovered how emotional intelligence is an anchor amidst the sea of virtual connections, enabling us to lead remote teams with compassion and efficacy.

We, project managers, are now armed with more knowledge of the emotional intelligence superpower; we stride confidently into the future—where challenges are opportunities, and success is measured in achievements and in the lasting impact we leave on those we lead.

Thank you for reading this book! As you embrace your role as an emotionally intelligent project manager, may your projects flourish, and may you inspire a legacy of emotional intelligence in all aspects of your life.

If you find it in your heart to leave a good review, it will help others find this book, and it would greatly be appreciated!

About the Author

Dr. Oborsk is a Project Management Office Director, Program Manager, Blogger, Color Code Personality Trainer, and emotional intelligence practitioner and enthusiast. He brings over 20 years of experience in leadership and project management and is always willing to dive deep into how emotional intelligence can improve project management.

A native Ukrainian speaker, Stefan resides in greater Tampa, Florida, with his wife and two daughters.

To find out more about him or connect with him directly, make sure to check out his LinkedIn profile:

https://www.linkedin.com/in/dr-stefan-oborski-d-mgmt-79b9304/

Or contact him via email at:

stefan@theemotionallyintelligentPM.com

Made in the USA
Monee, IL
03 January 2025

75774484R00075